ENGLISH CROWN GRANTS

ENGLISH CROWN GRANTS

The Foundation
of Colonial Land Titles
Under English Common Law

by

S. L. Mershon

MEMBER OF
THE NATIONAL GEOGRAPHIC SOCIETY, WASHINGTON, D.C.; NEW YORK HISTORICAL
SOCIETY, NEW YORK CITY; CITY HISTORY CLUB, NEW YORK CITY;
STATEN ISLAND INSTITUTE OF ARTS AND SCIENCES;
STATEN ISLAND ANTIQUARIAN SOCIETY

AUTHOR OF
The Major and the Queen
(A NARRATIVE OF COLONIAL HISTORY)

HERITAGE BOOKS
2012

HERITAGE BOOKS

AN IMPRINT OF HERITAGE BOOKS, INC.

Books, CDs, and more—Worldwide

For our listing of thousands of titles see our website
at
www.HeritageBooks.com

A Facsimile Reprint
Published 2012 by
HERITAGE BOOKS, INC.
Publishing Division
100 Railroad Ave. #104
Westminster, Maryland 21157

--- Publisher's Notice ---
In reprints such as this, it is often not possible to remove blemishes from
the original. We feel the contents of this book warrant its reissue despite
these blemishes and hope you will agree and read it with pleasure.

International Standard Book Numbers
Paperbound: 978-0-7884-0281-4
Clothbound: 978-0-7884-9135-1

CONTENTS

FOREWORD

The American Bar Associations, Historical Societies, Colonial Organizations and all thoughtful citizens have a vital interest in the unique history and present-day dominating influence, in America, of the old English Crown Grants.

Their virility is unimpaired despite the flight of centuries.

The Royalty of the past frequently restricts and restrains the Democracy of to-day.

It was the personal will and whim of the English Sovereigns, as expressed in the English Crown Grants, that prescribed the basis of Governmental, Commercial, Educational and Industrial Institutions, in the American Colonies, which Colonies subsequently constituted "the Original Thirteen States."

English Crown Grants are to-day powerfully active elements in our National Life.

Great Universities, including Yale and Princeton, many ancient and wealthy churches, sit tight and smug under powers received by them, in their charters, from autocratic hands now long since crumbled into dust.

Ferries are now operating in New York because English Kings, centuries ago granted the franchises so to do. Competition therewith is restrained because the olden time and long since deceased monarchs decreed that such Ferries should constitute a monopoly.

FOREWORD

The most powerful title company in the world has recently announced that it will not guarantee its land title searches covering lands in one of the Boroughs of Greater New York, if required to make such searches back to the English Crown Grants.

Every foot of land, in that designated Borough depends, for a complete chain of title, upon some one basic Grant from the English Crown.

To ignore that fact is fatalistic, to defy it is recklessness, especially in the face of the indictment of the land titles of an entire Borough of Greater New York by the world's most powerful title company.

Incredible disregard of the rights descending under English Crown Grants, confirmed by treaty between Great Britain and the United States of America, which treaties are " the supreme law of the land," has precipitated costly litigation involving vast areas of lands of immense values in the Borough of the Bronx, on Riverside Drive, at Coney Island, Rockaway Beach, Oyster Bay, Northport, Lake Champlain, the Hudson River and many other places in New York State.

Like controversies have involved land titles in Maryland, Delaware, Virginia and other States.

The uniform and inflexible attitude of both Federal and State Courts has been to sustain the legality and inviolability of the English Crown Grants as covering lands Granted by the English Crown in the American Colonies.

The English Crown Grants of lands on Staten Island have been selected by the author as the most diversified, yet favorable grouping of Grants, to illustrate the discussion of the problems involved.

FOREWORD

Probably no locality in English Colonial America furnishes such an interesting, varied and yet complete group of Crown Grants as appears on the public records of Richmond County, New York, in which County Staten Island is situated.

S. L. MERSHON.

Montclair, N. J.

THE PSYCHOLOGY

OF

CROWN GRANTS

WHAT IS LAW? Many have been the responses to this query. It has been said that law is composed of three elements:—

FIRST:—A command of the lawgiver, which command must prescribe, not a single act merely, but a series or class of acts.

SECOND:—An obligation imposed thereby on a citizen.

THIRD:—A sanction threatened in the event of disobedience. (Benth. Frag. on Gov.)

Blackstone defines law as:

"A rule of civil conduct prescribed by the "Supreme Power in the State, commanding what "is right and prohibiting what is wrong." (1 B. La. Com. 44.)

"The law of the land as used in the Magna "Charta and adopted in many of the earlier "constitutions of the original Thirteen States "means more than the Legislative will. It re- "quires the due and orderly proceeding of Jus-

1

"tice, according to the established methods."
(8 Gray 29.)

In the United States, the organic law of a State is termed the Constitution, and the term "laws" generally designate Statutes or Legislative Enactments in contradistinction to the Constitution.

> "Law, as distinguished from equity, denotes
> "the doctrine and procedure of the common law
> "of England and America, from which equity
> "is a departure."

Human reason demanded the enunciation of the incontrovertible principles upon which the temple of justice might be reared. Constitutional authorities are in agreement that the true source of all law from which equity and justice flow is in the immutable, unchangeable and all-powerful will of God, permeating and extending throughout all nature and dominating and controlling all life.

We find, therefore, in its final analysis, or shorn of all confusing and complex definitions that law finds its true interpretation in the correct answer to that ever-recurring question, "What is Truth?" Truth is the rule of "Exact accordance with that which is, or has been, or shall be." as developed by that Supreme Power which makes for Righteousness. In recognition of this generic principle, a Court of Justice is designed to discover the truth. Witnesses are sworn in the presence of the Supreme Soverign to declare "the truth, the whole truth and nothing but the truth." The Divine Master, when he would cleanse Humanity from its corruption, put up the petition to the Almighty Father, "Sanctify them through Thy Truth, Thy Word is Truth." This was an invocation that the laws of Divine Justice might find ramification throughout all human relations, the culmination of which would be "Peace on earth, good will to men." The highest consummation of all law is the rule of the "law of love." "Law is beneficence acting by rule." "Love is the fulfillment of the Law."

It is a trite saying that in the bosom of every acorn there lies dormant the form and pattern of a majestic oak. Stricken by the winter's cold, forced into action by the summer's heat, and drinking at the font of evening showers, the acorn hears the call of life and starts on its upward toilsome, yet unconscious climb for the fulfillment of the marvelous design of which it has been made the sacred shrine. Law anticipated its being, co-ordinated its elements and having charged its life with a design, which of necessity presupposes a dominating, directing and governing intelligence, sent if forth on its beneficent mission of tree building. Every tree represents a Super-Intelligence, directing and guiding a subservient force, working out an engineering design, embodying mechanical construction and chemical processes, along lines of artistic skill and beauty; and all with special adaptation to human needs. Under its shade we may rest and contemplate but never duplicate it by our artifice.

A tree is not a thesis in the school of human thought. It is an axiom. It is a bound volume in nature's law library, indexing, by its trunk, branches, leaves, blossoms and fruit, the intelligent purpose, organizing power and beneficent operation of an intelligent law that works in nature's arena of human activities.

That masterful, dominating Intelligence "that was, is, and is to be," and which is the Creator and Director of the forces of Nature, the royal sway of which tends to the highest good and greatest happiness, has not confined the implanting of His law within the bounds of unintelligent nature. We find in embryonic form in the minds of men everywhere an endowed tendency which when given its true opportunity for development, works out the highest system of justice in human relations.

"The Ancients said their laws came from the "gods. The Cretons attributed their laws, not "to Minos but to Jupiter. The Lacedaemonians "believed that their legislator was not Lucurgus, "but Apollo. The Romans believed that Numa "wrote under the direction of one of the most "powerful divinities of ancient Italy,—the god- "dess Egeria. The Etruscans had received their "laws from the god Tages.

"There is truth in all these traditions. The "veritable legislator among the ancients was not "a man but the religious belief which men enter- "tained. The laws long remained sacred.

"From this we can understand the respect and "attachments which the ancients long had for "their laws. In them they saw no human work, "but one whose origin is holy. It was no vain "word when Plato said, 'To obey the laws is to "obey the gods.'

"In principle, the laws were immutable, since
"they were divine.

"Man did not need to study his conscience
"and say, 'This is just and this is unjust.' An-
"cient law was not produced in that way. But
"man believed that the sacred hearth, in virtue
"of the religious law, passed from father to son;
"from this it followed that the house was hered-
"itary property. The man who had buried his
"father in his field believed that the spirit of the
"dead one took possession of this field forever
"and required a perpetual worship of his pos-
"terity. As a result of this, the field, the domin-
"ion of the dead and place of sacrifice, became
"the inalienable property of the family.

"Religion said 'the son continues the worship,
"not the daughter; and the law said, with the
"religion, 'the son inherits, the daughter does not
"inherit, but not the nephew on the female side.'

"This was the manner in which the laws were
"made; they presented themselves without being
"sought. They were the direct and necessary
"consequence of the belief; they were religion it-
"self applied to the relations of men among
"themselves." (Primitive and Ancient Institutions, pages 106, 107.)

The American Indian, in order to express Sovereignty, used the word "Sachem," which being interpreted, means "Power from above." The Peruvian
aborigines declared that their Incas were the children
of their divinity, the Sun.

"The Laws of the Medes and Persians changeth

not," they being as was then believed to be divine decrees, which were "the same yesterday, to-day, and forever."

According to the Greeks, the sacred fire taught men to build houses. The house was always placed in the sacred enclosure. The walls were raised around the sacrificial hearth to isolate and defend it, and it was the religion of the family that influenced the erection of the house. The house was consecrated by the perpetual presence of the gods. It was the temple idea which preserved them.

> "Here is his altar, here is his hearth, here are
> "his household gods; here all his sacred rights,
> "all his religious ceremonies are preserved."

Family tombs, walled in, gradually gave rise to individual title to lands. The dead were gods, the object of family worship, and their burial places, through religion, became family properties with title from the gods.

The militant spirit conceived the house to be a man's "citadel." The religious instinct gave birth to the doctrine of the "sacred" rights of proprietorship in a homestead.

We of this generation have inherited from our ancestors the doctrine that the original and ultimate title to all property was and is vested in the King, Queen or other Sovereign power. This theory is explainable in several ways as it developed among our different ancestral tribes. They all hark back, however, to the principle implanted in the universal mind of man, that all property rights and titles originally vested in and eminated from the Supreme

Sovereign of all the Universe. That by the free and voluntary act of the Omnipotent Ruler, lands were apportioned among the children of men. "The Most High divided to the Nations their inheritance." (Ex. 32:8.) Such lands, however, when so apportioned carried therewith "the obligation of fealty and service" to the Great King. Titles having been so conveyed to His subjects, the obligation "followed with the land," so that the Grantees when called upon should appear, in feudal fashion, as loyal retainers and true soldiers of the King to do moral battle for Him. Such a Royal Grant from the Great Sovereign required that the King's Grantee should justly, by gift and bequest, apportion lands among others on like "conditions of fealty and service" to the King. Thus the King's realm would be safe and his subjects happy. To accept and serve under allegiance to such a divine government is to establish a well-ordered rule of righteousness.

This doctrine of original proprietorship and ultimate ownership of all land as being vested in the Supreme Sovereign of all the earth is most clearly represented in its purest form in the History of the Hebrew Race. Their representative, Moses, went up into Mount Sinai and received their Laws for them, direct from the unseen and invisible Ruler of all the Universe. They receive their Grant to the land "beyond Jordan" from that same Imperial Source—"The land which the Lord thy God giveth thee." (Ex. 20:12.) They entered and took possession thereof according to the terms of the Grant. By Imperial decree they evicted the prior owners because the latter had not paid their proper quit rents of fealty and service to the Great King from whom they had received the land. Such land, however, so seized and possessed by the Hebrews was still charged with the obligation of fealty and service to Jehovah and was taken over by the twelve tribes of Israel with full knowledge of and consent to the conditions imposed thereon.

The tithing tax appears in the well-known Hebraic code of laws. The Hebrews received and held the title to the divinely granted land, but the original and ultimate ownership was admittedly in their recognized but Unseen Sovereign, and their tenure thereof was a conditional one. They had a title subject to forfeiture, for the Sovereign did subsequently re-enter, taking possession thereof and evicted them from the land when they violated their oath of allegiance, or pledge of fealty to Him, and paid their tribute to other kings or deities. The true proprietor of the lands had, however, duly served advance notice upon them and upon their continued default he escheated the lands. The doctrine of Original Proprietorship and Ultimate Ownership of title by the Supreme Ruler was thereafter re-enunciated when the true Heir to the Throne subsequently appeared in the lands which were still possessed by Israel under the above mentioned Grant. Meanwhile the Romans had levied upon the land in true sheriff fashion and eviction was then pending.

Jesus Christ, the Crown Prince of Israel, came to restore, if possible, the original relationship between His Father, the Proprietor, and His about to be dispossessed subjects. He patiently explained to the people His Father's right thereto by telling them that

"All things were made by Him, and without Him was not anything made that was made." He further confirmed to them the statement of their own beloved over-lord, King David, who had said that "The earth is the Lord's and the fulness thereof." In this way they were called upon to see that both real estate and personal property, as to ultimate ownership and original proprietorship were vested in the Great King, or Jehovah. In remarkable imagery, so dear to the heart of every Hebrew, this Prince explained to them how the lands had been apportioned out as if the soil was a great "vineyard," while "the owner went into a far country." He gave them to understand their possessory rights, in the well-known term, "occupy until I come." The Hebrews were given to understand that a renewed grant and continued possession were due to the *"profitable* servant" while dispossession would be justly meted out to the *"unprofitable* servant." He distinctly told them that upon the Great Sovereign's demand for an accounting the Sovereign had a right to expect that He was "to receive His own, with interest." The enunciation of this principle drew out of the rich young man the avowal, "I give tithes of all I possess." (Luke 18:12.) In American Colonial language, it might well have been stated, "I always pay my quit rents to the Great King of Heaven and Earth."

This Royal Crown Prince further laid down another and very broad principle that is wider than its application to the Hebrew race. In its scope it is as broad as humanity, and in point of time extends to the limits of human life. He made it plain that all properties, both real and personal, having originally

issued forth from the Great Proprietor, will ultimately revert to that Great Proprietor, and that the
ultimate dispossession of the entire human race from
this planet will, as is now predicted by science, restore
complete title and possession to the original, sole and
true owner, "the King of all the Earth." God in his
earthly solitude will then watch at the grave where
the last human sleeps. He it was who held in one
vast unbroken estate the solitudes of Earth before
Eden heard the footfalls of human life. From him
issued the Grants of land to the people whom He
created and for whom the world was prepared. A
great purpose inspired it and great moral obligations
were imposed.

> The world's greatest law giver, Moses, said,
> "And all the tithes of land, whether the
> "seed of the land or the fruit of the trees, is the
> "Lord's; it is holy unto the Lord." (Lev. 27:
> 30.) That is to say, the "Quit Rents" are
> wholly His, and the obligations for the payment
> thereof "run with the land."

This doctrine is basic in the realm of human
thought. It has developed the legal maxim current
in text books of law. "It is more serious to hurt divine than temporal majesty." (2 Cor. 29.) Therefore, we swear our witnesses in the presence of the
Ever Living God, while they hold the Book of His
Law in their hands.

Among the races of men who originally accepted
the theocratic form of government as fundamentally
correct were some with materialistic tendencies. They
revolted against straining their eyes towards an in-

visible Sovereign. Their minds recoiled against an immaterial and invisible government. Mental, moral and spiritual forces were, to their sordid vision, as nothing in comparison with burnished steel and sharpened lances. A "Commission form of government" residing in a Board of Judges, when put to the test broke down among the Jews and the Hebrews cried out for a king. The spirit of militarism then ran high among them. Jehovah, they thought, was in another world. The prophets and the judges, they concluded, were wise old men, but somewhat passeé and without force to back up their decrees. Hence they cried, "Give us a king." Then there promptly appeared among them the wily politician and ambitious soldiers, who were ready for political place and power.

Had not Moses, the autocrat, delivered to the people the very laws of Heaven? The prophets and judges had seemed to the Jews quasi divine. Why then should not a human king of earth voice the decrees of the King of Heaven and back them up with military, in place of spiritual forces?

It is impossible in the short space of this statement to trace from its concept to its conclusion the amazing and now almost inconceivable doctrine of "the divine right of kings." "The King can do no wrong." (2 Rolle 304; Jenk Cent 9-3); Boom Max 52; Sharsw. Bla. Com. 246.) "The King never dies." (Boom Max 50; Branch Max 5th Ed. 197; Bla Com. 259.) "The King cannot deceive or be deceived." (Grounds and Rud. of Law 439.)

This idealized but false conception of the earthly king's perfection was sporadic, infectious and became universal. To the earthly king as successor to the Divine Sovereign therefore fell the proprietorship of all "the vacant and unappropriated lands within the realm." To him fealty must be pledged. To him the revenue must be paid. Divinity dethroned. Humanity enthroned—"Long live the King."

Among the prerogatives of sovereignty, conscription was a "Divine right." Even in these modern days, when the tides of democracy are sweeping with tremendous force about the thrones of Imperial rulers, we hear enunciated, in royal proclamations under the seal of the Crown, such expressions as "My realm," "My kingdom," "My army," "My navy," and "My people." The doctrine of Original Proprietorship and Ultimate Ownership in the *human* sovereign exists today with tremendous force and power. It is recognized to the fullest extent in international law and stands convicted at the bar of Public Opinion as the primal cause of the horrible tragedies being enacted in the world war, the scourge of Europe, and the atheist of a heart-broken world.

Divine Sovereignty, as revealed in a true Christian Socialism is day by day steadily and gradually coming into its own. Mark the term, however, *Christian* Socialism.

The tragic attempt on the part of humanity to depose Divine sovereignty and to impose in its place a human king, with Divine prerogatives and powers is pathetically illustrated in the prophetic narrative (1 Sam., Chap. 8), from which we make the following citations:

"Then all the elders of Israel gathered them-

"selves together and came to Samuel at Ramah,
"and said unto him, Now make us a king to
"judge us like all the nations.

"But the thing displeased Samuel, when they

"said Give us a king to judge us. And Samuel
"prayed unto the Lord.

"And the Lord said unto Samuel, hearken
"unto the voice of the people in all that they say
"unto thee, for they have not rejected thee, but
"they have rejected me, that I should not reign
"over them . . . Howbeit yet protest solemnly
"unto them and show them the manner of the
"king that shall reign over them. And Samuel
"told all the words of the Lord unto the people
"that asked of him a king.

"Nevertheless the people refused to obey the
"voice of Samuel and they said, Nay, but we will
"have a king over us."

Divine Majesty was dethroned! Then human sovereignty failed, dispossession of lands followed, and Israel wandered a scattered nation, without a country. That most marvelous of all people, the Hebrews, are now being restored to their own home land, such restitution having been made possible by the great World Powers under the spiritual leadership of that man of all men, that Jew of all Jews, Jesus the Son of David, the climax of all prophecy and the incarnation of "the hope of Israel."

Fealty and service will again be required by Jehovah as a condition precedent to renewed possession of this "Holy Land," which was apportioned to the children of Israel when "the Most High divided to the Nation's their inheritance." (Ex. 32 : 8.)

Then shall "the wailing places of the Jews" be flooded with song as the erstwhile escheated land of sacred and sorrowful memories shall once again resound with the songs of Israel. He who asserts an absolute title in himself to any land whatsoever and claims that the same is exempt from "the obligation of fealty and service" to the Great Sovereign will eventually be adjudged as in default. His land will be finally escheated and he himself will be at last evicted from the Crown Estate for general default, under the terms of the Original Crown Grant. To him who denies fealty to the Highest and evades his true obligations, "the tax dodger of two worlds," the record speaks:

"But God said unto him, Thou fool, this night "thy soul shall be required of thee: then whose "shall those things be which thou hast provided?

"So is he that layeth up treasures for himself and is not rich towards God." (Luke 12 :20, 21.)

"It is a mistake to think ourselves stewards in some of God's gifts and proprietors in others."

THE EVOLUTION

OF

CROWN GRANTS

It has well been said that in the early ages of the world the condition of the land was probably allodial; that is, it was not subject to any superior. Every man occupied as much land found unappropriated as his necessities required. Over this land he exercised an unqualified dominion. This condition reminds us of the original Adam in the Garden of Eden, who for a time did not even possess a wife to claim "a dower" in the lands beneath his feet, and a Robinson Crusoe "whose rights there was none to dispute."

Blackstone did not accept the theory that in the earlier stages of the human race man wandered about alone and in vast solitudes. He believed that fear of the unknown and a sense of human need caused them to group themselves together in their wanderings.

When the armies of Cæsar were penetrating the forest vastnesses of northern Europe, the Teutonic people were being gradually transformed from nomadic tribes into settlers in small villages and hamlets, with fixed habitations. Nomadic groups of people, upon arriving at a river or seaside, favorable for fishing, acquired the habit of settling there at least for a time. Others, upon reaching a rich and luxurious valley well adapted for herding or tilling would there

15

erect crude huts and make permanent their stay. Human wanderers, perchance pursued by thievish and hostile foes, upon reaching land easily defended, would there form a simple but definite settlement.

These villages or permanent encampments, were the first foundation stones, uncut, rough and un-symmetrical, which formed the original basis of modern rights of land ownership among Teutonic peoples and their descendants. Out from such a crude and rugged source has flowed one of the gradual but ever widening streams of land titles, forming a part of the present day codified rights of ownership in real-estate in Teutonic countries. This theory was the antipode of the one according to which land was acquired in the original American Colonies.

As civilization advanced from these primitive conditions society became more complex. Every upward step developed greater needs. Accumulated wealth and broader culture imperatively called for added security, comfort and civic order, until at the present time we are surrounded by conditions, regulated and controlled by statutes and laws, protecting property rights, guarding human life, also defining and guaranteeing personal liberty. All these are the natural and logical developement of a system called into existence by human progress, and calculated from actual experience to safeguard human rights.

The communities referred to were at first generally composed of kinsfolk in households, or a cluster of families. The bonds binding the members of the settlements were either those of kinship or a recognized need for mutual defense and protection.

As these small, primitive colonies developed among the Teutonic tribes certain questions at once arose in each as to the rights of the respective householders to the soil on which they had pitched their tents, erected their camps, enclosed their flocks or herds, or upon which they were cultivating their needed vegetable or grain supplies.

At first in all such primitive communities certain "land marks" or lines were drawn upon the ground through the settlements and a general understanding was arrived at by mutual and oral consent, that within the confines of the land so marked out the respective householders alone had sway. It was at first but a possessory right pending the period of occupancy.

The theory appears to have been that he who occupied such land had but the use of the land so plotted out and did not have any actual ownership in the land itself. As time passed on and families remained established at fixed points, houses replacing huts, the theory of "occupancy for use" gradually developed into a claim of ownership of the soil on which the domicil had been erected. This right of proprietorship being once established, there naturally developed the right of sale of such property so held.

In this manner there were gradually established first villages and then townships in which the houses and what pertained thereto were distinguished as individual properties. What had once been communal dwellings were recognized as fixed habitations and became the abode of separate and distinct families, dwelling upon land representing individual proprietorships.

These local settlements were but oases in great

expanses of forests, hills and dales, which were considered to be "No Man's Land," and over which waste places no human sovereign ruled. Such wild and vacant lands were imagined to be largely possessed by hybred and nondescript creatures, which were in fact born of human superstition and ignorant fear of the indefinite and unknown. Demonology and witchcraft held sway therein and the popular deities in those vast expanses were conjured up demons.

Under these primitive conditions, house property in villages and towns was generally regarded as having an absolutely independent and separate character from properties located in the agricultural and pastoral outskirts of the villages. The latter were considered to be the common lands of the community. From this communal theory of lands so held we inherit what we now term "The Commons."

At first little regard was had for individual rights of ownership in cultivatable soil, as agriculture being but crudely and carelessly developed, was of an uncertain and changeable nature.

A piece of land selected by a householder for herding his flocks in one season, might be, and very frequently was, abandoned for another piece or patch of ground the following season. Thus it came about that while definite bounds were fixed for village and town habitations, as of individual proprietorship, the doctrine of lands-in-common, or "the commons" of later days became established.

In this way there gradually developed two principles of land ownership, known respectively as "folklands" or lands owned by individuals and common or communal lands which were owned by the people in common.

As human intelligence increased and the importance and value of definite locations became more fixed and determined, a system or method of regulating and defining individual rights and establishing orderly control of the communal properties became necessary.

Thereupon the custom came into vogue of entering in a book a description of the properties individually claimed and recognized by the community to be folk-land and which had become subject to private ownership.

From that time on such lands were known as "Book-land." The entries so made in such books became the recognized proofs and established the fact of individual proprietorship in the lands so recorded. These simple books of entry subsequently developed into our elaborate system of county records, brought down to us as a heritage from our early ancestors.

Upon frequent occasions members of these early communities desired the temporary use of certain of the commons or communal lands. These demands the communities were ready and willing to grant for a limited period of time, but subject to the reversion of such lands to the community and without altering the character of such lands.

When such permission was so given, proper entries were made in the same book and a record of such permission was entered and defined therein, duly setting forth the right of the lessee to use such lands for a temporary period but in no wise parting with or conveying to such individual or individuals the actual ownership of such communal soil.

From this latter custom has gradually developed the theory of communal leases, now in vogue and controlled by our elaborate system of legal enactments.

Generations came and went while wealth increased. Communities composed of various tribes differing in vocations and languages but equally charged with barbaric impulses multiplied. These groups came into close contact with each other; the friction of which contact resulted in frequent and fatal clashes. A sense of constant fear of attack and the danger of destruction pervaded communities which under more isolated conditions had rested in a reasonable sense of security.

Leadership in each community had been generally established by the selection of the physically most powerful and agressive warrior as chief. Later, alliances between weaker and neighboring communities as a common protection and defense against larger and more powerful neighbors became a necessity.

Thereupon strong, brave and daring leaders for such communal alliances were called for by developing conditions. This need, once realized and acted upon, rapidly transformed small states into kingdoms and empires.

Thus kings governing large states appeared in Teutonic history. They might not always supplant the local chieftains, whose authority through the vicissitudes of time and the expansion of territory was steadily magnified, but they could co-ordinate and direct them. These formerly independent but lesser chieftains gradually became the barons, lords and other petty rulers under great imperial sovereigns, called by the people to power or by warrior usurpers of the throne.

Whether this evolution from early to later conditions was generally due to the gradual development of national conditions or usually came through wars of conquest or internal strife is immaterial in this narrative of events. Such evolution or revolution has however much to do with the development of the rights of land ownership both by the people and the Crown.

Vivified and fostered by these national developments, the doctrine of the Crown ownership of lands evolved therefrom.

We have referred to the doctrine of individual proprietorship of land, which was actually possessed, as a gradually developed right of the individual householder.

We have shown communal lands, held in common by the community for the public's benefit and subject to lease or sale by the public authorities.

What of the vast area of vacant, unappropriated and waste land in the expanse of mountains, forests and valleys situated between the communities, but without ownership?

How was the king or sovereign to be provided for and what compensation was to be paid to him for his guardianship and protection of the various communities over which he had been called to rule?

The landed proprietors were naturally warriors: but when their services were placed at the disposal of the King for war, it was at least, in theory, in defense of their own properties, their families, and for their own booty and glory which they to a degree divided with their king.

Certain portions of private land, crops and other incomes and accumulated wealth, these land owners likewise pledged to their sovereign and king, but that was, in theory largely, to assist the sovereign in the support of armies which were enlisted for the defense of the confederated communities.

Why therefore, should not the wild, vacant and unappropriated lands become the property of the king, to be held absolutely as Crown property and not as communal lands? No individual owned them. No community claimed them. The title had never passed from the Creator and the King claimed his throne by Divine right.

From this theory of compensation to the sovereign who held to a large extent in his hands the safety of the community, grew to a degree the right of Crown ownership in and to all such lands so described.

We therefore find in the course of time that the great forests were recognized as the property of the Crown, and that the Crown controlled therein "the hunting and the hawking." We also find the navigable rivers spoken of as the "royal rivers," because of the fact that the sovereign owned the river bottoms of navigable streams as a part of the vast area of "the vacant and unappropriated lands" of the realm. "And he was the only one who could defend the same, by his mighty army and mighty fleet."

We also discover as a fully recognized fact of early English history and laws that the seas were "royal seas" and that the titles to the bottoms of the bays, seas and in fact the bottoms of all tidal waters in the realm were vested in the English Crown.

The universal existence of some form of proprietorship, law and government is a natural and fundamental concept of the well organized and balanced mind.

It will be seen that under colonial conditions, at the period of the American colonization, the King of England, by the natural descent, growth and development of a primitive legal system, which was brought to England from continental Europe, owned all the ungranted lands under navigable waters in the Thirteen Original American Colonies. The doctrine included Crown ownership of the vacant and unappropriated uplands, together with the fishery rights and the ungranted hawking and hunting privileges of the English realm. This Crown ownership in England was exclusive of folklands, communal lands and the private and communal rights there incident and pertaining thereto. The title to the communal lands in England was held by the Crown in trust for the people, but with power to grant the same.

It is a fundamental principle that the ultimate title of all lands of every kind and nature is vested in the Sovereign power. In monarchical countries that ultimate right is vested in the King, while in democratic countries it is vested in the legislative power, which represents the people.

The original and ultimate title of all lands vested in the Sovereign, rests upon the theory that he or it represents the Divine source of power and that the sovereign's life and property will always be available in the defense of the lives and property of his loyal subjects.

Blackstone enunciated this doctrine when he said, "The King is esteemed in the eyes of the law as the original proprietor of all the lands in the kingdom."

That principle is set forth by another authority as follows:

> "Under common law principles, all lands with-
> "in the state are held directly or indirectly by the
> "King as Lord paramount or supreme proprie-
> "tor: to him every occupant of the land owes
> "fidelity and service of some kind as the neces-
> "sary condition of his occupance."

The above theory holds in the United States and is but the re-affirmation of principles which prevail in England and in fact in all countries with well established legal systems. In America, however, the doctrine of the divine right of kings has been repudiated. The people have seized the seat and place of power. They enthroned, have held firmly to that higher allegiance typified by the national adage, "In God we trust."

It has been clearly stated by competent authorities that,

> "In this country the people in their corporate
> "capacity represent the state sovereignty. Every
> "man must bear true allegiance to the State and
> "pay his share of the taxes required for her sup-
> "port, as the condition upon which alone he may
> "hold land within her boundaries."

This right of ultimate ownership in the sovereign

is not simply a theory of political economy, but is most clearly, frequently and very drastically put into force and effect in all civilized countries, so that its practical character is now indisputable.

A citizen who violates the supreme law of the land may not only be restrained of his personal liberty, but as a further penalty, his property, both real and personal, may be forfeited to the State, as the supreme power.

When a citizen is guilty of treason against the Government under which he resides and to which he owes allegiance, his life may not only be forfeited but his lands and personal property may also be escheated to the State.

If a man dies without making proper disposal, by will, of his real and personal property, and if at the same time such person has no blood relatives or natural heirs, all of his property immediately reverts to the State as the ultimate owner or proprietor.

In fact, a citizen's right to inherit and his right to bequeath are but statuary rights and privileges, which, if repealed would in one generation vest the title to all property in the Sovereign power.

It has been stated as a fact of history and it has also been judicially determined by the American and English courts of last resort that,

> "The American Colonists brought with them "from England the English Common Law and "Code, in so far as the same were adapted to the "conditions on the American continent. (Grant "by Charles II, King of England, to James, the "Duke of York and Albany, on March 12th, "1664).

To what extent early American conditions might have modified the Common Law practice of England, when the same was applied in the Western Hemisphere, is readily ascertained by reference to the numerous decisions of the English and Provincial Courts, during the American Colonial period prior to the Revolutionary War. Such decisions are remarkably in harmony with the very clear and lucid deliverances of the American State and Federal Courts, subsequent to the Revolution, when judicially passing upon questions involving English and American Common law.

STATEN ISLAND

AND

CROWN GRANTS

The English Crown claimed the lands on the Atlantic coast covered by Sebastian Cabot's discovery. International law fully concedes this claim which vested jurisdiction over the lands in the English Crown by the right of discovery.

There has been much discussion as to what extent the English Crown owned Colonial lands as its own private property and to what extent the English Crown held such land in trust for the people.

There has been considerable flexibility in the judicial decisions as to where the Crown private ownership ended and the Crown Trusteeship commenced. No authority denies the right of private ownership by the Crown in Crown lands, or the fact of ownership of other lands in England by the Crown in trust for the people. Where is the line of demarkation to be drawn?

Be that as it may, certain facts stands out clearly, distinctly and prominently in connection with Crown lands in the State of New York and particularly as to the Crown lands of Staten Island. No ambiguity or uncertainty can prevail as to the regularity and legality of the English Crown Grants made to lands in the State and especially on Staten Island.

Using Staten Island as an illustration of the exercise of the English Sovereign Power in the making of Crown Grants, the facts and circumstances relating thereto furnish probably the best and most complete example of English Crown Grants which can be drawn from Colonial history.

Staten Island was included in the Cabot Discovery which gave dominion to the English Crown by right of discovery. Staten Island was included in the conquered territory obtained by the English in the war with the Dutch, which gave political sovereignty over Staten Island to the English Crown, by the right of conquest.

Thereupon the English, as was their invariable custom in America, recognized the Indian inhabitants of Staten Island as,

"The very true, sole and lawful Indian own-
"ers of ye said island," and
"as derived to them by their ancestors."

The Duke of York, who subsequently became James II, King of England, by a fair bargain and for good and valuable considerations, purchased, on April 13th, 1670, the soil of Staten Island from the Indian inhabitants. The terms of that fair and equitable bargain were fully explained and the same were well understood by the native Indians. That honorable and very business like transaction gave title to the Duke of York by the right of purchase.

The ceremony carried out in connection with the said purchase is fully set forth in "THE MAJOR AND THE QUEEN", (page 12) and need not be referred to herein, excepting only to show that the

Indians received full, complete and satisfactory payment therefor, after which they vacated Staten Island without a murmer, giving to the English full and complete possession thereof (THE MAJOR AND THE QUEEN, page 16).

It may be referred to as a further interesting fact that for many years thereafter and on or about the anniversary of the sale above mentioned, surviving representatives of the Indian tribes, which had delivered possession of Staten Island to the English, called upon the Crown representatives in Manhattan and reaffirmed their satisfaction with the sale so made and their continued friendship for the English Crown.

When James the Duke of York, succeeding his brother, Charles II, became James II, King of England, Staten Island, which he had purchased of the Indians, became a portion of the private estate of the English Crown, or private Crown lands.

It would be utterly impossible to frame a single possible objection to the perfect and complete private title to Staten Island received and held by the Duke of York and retained by him as personal Crown land when he ascended the throne of England. He owned Staten Island before he became King and his inheritance of the Crown from his brother could by no means work a forfeiture of title to lands which he had previously purchased, nor could it automatically merge the King's personal title into that of the State.

After the purchase of Staten Island from the Indians and the accession of the Duke of York to the throne of England, English Crown land Grants were made in due form, to various individuals and covering every acre of land on Staten Island, "with-

in the bounds and limits of the County of Richmond."
The Grants were always made as of the Crown's private "Manor of East Greenwich, in the County of Kent, England," of which Manor Staten Island formed a part.

The boundaries of Staten Island and the boundaries of Richmond County in the State of New York have always been coextensive.

These boundaries were originally established by the English Government and subsequently by the states of New York and New Jersey in co-operation with the Federal Government.

There is not one square foot within those boundaries that was not the subject matter of and which was not clearly included in a good and valid English Crown Grant.

The records of the State of New York, as herein before stated, disclose a large number of Crown Grants of Staten Island lands, issued to various parties. These Grants, exclusive of the last and final Grant, were originally intended to cover about one half of Staten Island. The last, final and inclusive Grant, issued to Lancaster Symes, covered all of the remaining lands on Staten Island, together with various rights appertaining thereto and at that time belonging to the English Crown and which had been purchased of the Indians by the Duke of York on April 13th, 1670.

Each and every Grant by the English Crown, of lands on Staten Island, provided in effect by its terms that the lands so granted should be "Hold-in of us our heirs and successors in free and common soccage as of our Manor of East Greenwich, in the County of Kent, within our realme of England."

This final Grant to Lancaster Symes, was issued by the Crown itself in the person of Queen Anne and was confirmed by the Council and by the Governor General of the Province of New York. It was afterwards ratified and confirmed by the State of New York. (1816).

The Grant made to Lancaster Symes closed out to him all of the remaining rights of the English Crown in land both above and below the water on Staten Island and within the limits and bounds of Richmond County in the State of New York, excepting only the ultimate ownership of the Crown in the lands as Sovereign and the right to receive quit-rents from and under the Crown Grants issued.

It should be borne in mind that each and every Crown Grant made by the English Sovereign to lands on Staten Island was subject to the payment of annual quit-rents by the Grantee to the Crown.

These quit-rents though payable, for convenience, in New York City, were in fact a part of the Crown's private income from its Manor of East Greenwich in the County of Kent in England.

The officials of the English Government were originally the house servants of the English Crown. They gradually assumed the duties of public officials. Hence the Crown's personal accounts were kept in the books of State under the doctrine of "My Government,"—"My people."

These facts of history should satisfy any inquirer as to the complete and perfect title originally vesting in the English Crown, and its supreme right and

power to retain, lease or sell any part or all of Staten
Island as fully and freely as it could any part or all
of its Manor of East Greenwish in the County of
Kent, England, of which it formed a part, or as any
other property holder had the right to do with his
own *personal manorial property* or real estate.

Blackstone said, "The Third Right inherent in
every Englishman is that of property, which consists
in the free use, enjoyment and disposal of all his ac-
quisitions, without any control or diminuition, save
only the laws of the land." If the old proverb be
true that "a servant is not greater than his Lord,"
surely it must be true that a sovereign has at least
equal rights with his servant in his own personal estate.

The consideration for the final Grant by the
Crown to Lancaster Symes was ample. The combined power and authority of the Crown, the Provinces and the Council were represented in the Grant
to Lancaster Symes and to his heirs and assigns forever. It is conclusive on the theory that the English
Crown held the lands as a part of its own personal
estate as Crown lands; also on the false theory that it
held the same as Crown lands in trust for the English
People. The Grant to Lancaster Symes was issued by
both Crown and people and its validity is incontestable. It was subsequently ratified and confirmed by
the State of New York upon the commutation of
quit-rents thereunder by the State. (See Books of
Quits-Rents, State Comptroller's office, Albany,
Docket 48, page 106.)

Furthermore the English Crown had most certainly
the right to make the Grant to Lancaster Symes under

the title which obtained by purchase from the Indian inhabitants, there having been paid therefor a large and mutually satisfactory purchase consideration. The personal purchase from the Indian owners by the Duke of York had added Staten Island to the personal estate of the English Crown. It was at all times held thereafter as of the Crown Manor of East Greenwich, England.

In fact each and every Grant made by the English Crown on Staten Island is based upon as solid foundations as were or could be laid to colonial titles.

The issue of the Lancaster Symes Grant by the Crown, its confirmation under the Great Seal of the Province of New York and its reaffirmation through commutation of quit-rents by the State of New York renders the Grant incontestable.

During several centuries prior to the American Revolution the precise relation of the Crown to various classes of what were then designated as Crown lands, varied in accordance with the supremacy from time to time of the monarchical or democratic influences in governmental control of the affairs of England.

It is, however, a singular fact that during the reigns of the various sovereigns from 1670 to 1776 A. D., and notwithstanding the many changes of English dynasties, the attitude of Parliament and the decisions of the Higher courts of England relating to Colonial Crown lands, were in accord with the general principles of crown ownership of lands which prevailed at the time of the separation of the American Colonies from Great Britain.

It should be constantly borne in mind by the student of Crown Grants and by all persons interested in the descent of titles therefrom, that rights obtained under any Grant made by the English Crown to lands in America must be determined by the English common law governing the same at the time of such issue.

In other words, every Crown Grant must be read and construed under the customs prevailing at the time of its issue, and its verbiage must be interpreted and construed according to the then legal force and effect of the words and phrases used at the time of the Grant.

This doctrine has been repeatedly enunciated by the American Courts, as judicial opinions have harked back to and have defined and determined the rights and privileges intended to be and actually conveyed by the Crown at the time of the issue by it of Colonial Crown Grants in America.

In no case brought to bar in any of our American Courts relating to English Crown Grants has the following state of facts been fully involved and *pleaded,* and which is true of Staten Island Grants.

1st—That the English Crown (Charles II) made a Crown Grant to James, Duke of York, covering and including the lands in question, with the quit-rents payable to the Crown's private Manor of East Greenwich, in the County of Kent, England.

2nd—That upon the death of Charles II, his brother the said James, Duke of York, inheritted as his personal property the said Manor of East Greenwich, thereby merging the title thereto into his personal estate, with the quit-rents payable thereto.

3rd—That prior to the Duke of York's ascension to his brother's throne, he had made a purchase of the lands in question from the Indian owners thereof, so that a perfect title in fee by right of purchase vested in him before he became sovereign. Hence upon his accession to the throne "the lands were the property of the King and not of the kingdom."

4th—That he, upon his accession to the throne as James II, king of England, and his successors granted all of the lands on Staten Island to private individuals, thereby conveying to various grantees,

    (a)   All of the personal Crown title thereto.

    (b)   Any Imperial title therein.

5th—That the Province of New York attached to said Grants its Great Seal, thereby binding it.

6th—That the State of New York, by the commutation of quit-rents confirmed and renewed the final Grant and is thereby estopped from traversing it.

7th—That the people had no rights therein, and had it been otherwise they were closed out by the act of the Province of the State of New York, and by the State of New York.

In the period of approximately one-half century during which all of the Staten Island Crown Grants were issued by the English Sovereigns, there were no changes in Parliamentary law or Royal Practice affecting the integrity of Crown titles or their issue. No changed attitude of the English Crown, no adverse decision of the English Courts, nor any recorded protests on the part of the Province of New York, appear of record affecting the title of any Staten Island lands Granted by the Crown.

No event of history or legal enactment altered or changed the character or legal force and effect of any of the Staten Island English Crown Grants between the dates of the first Grant issued and the final Grant to Lancaster Symes.

In other words, every one of such Crown Grants stands on a parity with the others as to the general authority under which it was issued, the legal construction to be put upon the terms, provisions and conditions specified therein and the legal effect of the language or verbiage used to limit and define the force and effect of each such instrument.

The English Crown in issuing from time to time, Grants to land on Staten Island did, however, vary to some extent the terms, provisions and conditions of the Grants so made by it.

This may be illustrated in the two English Crown Grants made by it to Christopher Billop in the years 1676 and 1687 respectively.

In the first one of these Grants, Christopher Billop was granted a large tract of upland on a part of which Tottenville is now situated. This Grant was clearly intended to be an upland Grant and extended to high-water mark. This latter limitation evidently proved unsatisfactory to Billop and for apparently a very good reason which grew out of his life's occupation.

Christopher Billop was a sailor and as shown in the book entitled "THE MAJOR AND THE QUEEN" (and in other more elaborate and very excellent histories of Staten Island,—by Ira K. Morris, R. M. Bayles and J. H. Clute) Billop saved Staten Island for the Province of New York from the claims which New Jersey made upon it when the latter asserted that the Island geographically belonged to that Province.

This feat was accomplished when Billop demonstrated his ability to sail around Staten Island in twenty-four hours. The fact that Staten Island could be circumnavigated in that time brought Staten Island within the time limit of collections from the New York Custom House.

Christopher Billop was a sailor; his home was on land, but he loved and roved the seas. When the English Governor General rewarded Billop for his services in securing the claims of the Province of New York, by granting him land on Staten Island, it was natural that Billop should desire and receive the point of land extending farthest out into the waters and which by its location and outlook would appeal most to a sailor's heart.

When Billop received his first Grant, its limits and bounds on the waters were to high water mark. If Billop's lands extended only to high water mark, and Billop had undertaken to land his boat at low tide, he would have been a tresspasser upon the land between high and low water mark. Consequently at all times, excepting at high water, Billop would have been compelled to float his boat at sea waiting for the fullness of the tide to lawfully bring himself and his cargoes to shore. Nor could he construct a dock that would not have been "left high and dry" at ebb tide.

Such a situation practically placed an awkward barrier between the sailor's home and the sailor's ship. We learn, therefore, from the records that Billop obtained a second Grant from the Crown, which Grant covered all the lands previously granted by the Crown to Billop, but added considerable acreage thereto. This increase included favorable coves for the landing of boats west of the southern point of the Island and also Billop's lands *to low water mark*.

Under this latter arrangement Billop's Harbor facilities were greatly improved and his ability to bring to shore his boats on any and every tide was assured.

It is well to notice here that the English Crown changed the shore front lines for Billop because of the fact that there was a good and sufficient reason for it so to do. The change was one resulting from an expressed reason, was made upon due reflection and to meet an equitable demand based upon a commercial need.

No "riparian right" accrued or inured to Billop by which he could accept a Grant of the Crown's uplands and then compel the Crown to grant him more land on the shore. No such "Riparian right" inured to Billop as against the Crown, or to any other citizen in the British realm.

Especially is this indisputably true when it relates to lands privately purchased by the Duke of York of the Indians and added to the Crown's private lands against which no presumption of title could avail.

This denominated Riparian Right is a later doctrine applied to Staten Island by minds unacquainted with English Common Law in the Colonial period and the then rights of the English Crown. Staten Island was a part of the Crown's personal estate. It was property purchased. It was attached to a private Crown Manor. All Grants were construed favorably for the Crown and against the Grantee, excepting as shown herein in the "analysis of a Crown Grant."

The Monarchical theory as to the sacred rights of the King precluded a subject from receiving and accepting a Crown Grant of lands with fixed limitations and boundaries and then by implication asserting a lien or a "riparian right" to more of the Crown lands *than were included in the description contained in the Grant.* The lesser title, that of *the subject,* could not assert itself over the higher or greater title, that of *the Sovereign.*

While the Crown was in a generous mood, it dealt even more liberally with Billop than appears alone by acres and shore privileges. In the second Grant to him, it authorized, in elaborate detail, the founding or establishment for him of the Bentley Manor. The Crown Grants to Billop are interesting instruments and were issued along the lines consistent with the establishment of Manors in England.

While the founding of the Manor of Bentley was a departure as to jurisdiction from the ordinary Crown Grants issued on Staten Island, the authority to make the Grant, the interest given to Billop in the lands and the legal basis of the title to lands so granted to Billop, were the same as to all other lands granted on Staten Island. The authority given to Billop to exercise certain manorial rights and privileges within the limits and bounds of his Grant had no bearing whatever on the rights granted by the Crown to the lands underlying the same. The two are separate and distinct. Manorial rights are those of jurisdiction only, while land Grants are rights of proprietorship.

Manorial rights, privileges and authority were swept away by the triumphs of democracy in the American Revolution, but rights of property were not affected thereby.

Under the indisputable rights acquired by purchase from the Indian proprietors, Staten Island was owned in fee as personal Crown property.

Staten Island might have been held as a part of the private estate of the Crown, its title thereby descending from Sovereign to Sovereign, by right of personal inheritance in the same manner as the Crown descends. It might have been granted by the Crown to some one grantee of the Crown as a manor. This was done in the case of Gardiner's Island, at the East end of Long Island, by an English Crown Grant to Lyon Gardiner. This latter magnificent estate, so granted in its entirety, has descended from generation to generation in the Gardiner family even unto this day.

The English Crown, however, for the purpose of developing the Province of New York, as is clearly set forth by it in some of its Grants to lands on Staten Island, made Grants thereon to more than one hundred and fifty grantees, of which number the final and inclusive Grant was made to Lancaster Symes.

There are certain prominent and conspicuous features displayed in the various Grants issued by the Crown to lands on Staten Island. The lands in each case are especially described by metes and bounds, and the Grants are in themselves proof positive that the English Crown at that time, or during the period in which the series of Grants were issued, had a definite and accurate survey of Staten Island.

The many references to varying and natural features on the surface of the lands so granted, as shown in the respective Grants, clearly prove the Crown's intimate knowledge of the topography and exact location of such features on the surface of Staten Island.

This is in strange contrast with the expressed public opinion, prevailing for several generations past, to the effect that no survey by the English Crown had ever been made of Staten Island. In this case may not "the wish have been father of the thought" on the part of some who occupied lands, their titles to which could not be traced back to any English Crown Grant?

The theory that no survey of Staten Island was made in Colonial Days has been completely exploded by the investigation made through a long period of time and at large expense by the American Title and Trust Company, of Wilmington, Delaware, now so largely interested in property holdings on Staten Island.

This latter Company discovered in England and now has in its possession among its large collection of

Staten Island Maps, an English survey of Staten Island, made by the British Government prior to the American Independence showing the water fronts and uplands on Staten Island. It sets forth in varied and distinctive colors the then existing meadows, marshes, hills, highways, private roads, houses, lakes, ponds, bays, rivers and seas. The Map is drawn to scale and contains the compass and the then variation of the magnetic pole. It is a superb piece of workmanship and displays a painstaking care as to details which might well challenge the admiration and envy of the employees of many modern surveyor's offices were they called upon to duplicate this map by an original survey.

In addition to the important general survey referred to, the American Title and Trust Company has also secured from official sources a map of Staten Island prepared by Government officials and which map locates each and every English Crown Grant issued for lands on Staten Island.

Each Crown Grant is clearly defined thereon by metes and bounds. A compass and the variation of the magnetic needle is also clearly shown thereon.

In addition to the foregoing maps, the American Title and Trust Company has also sought out, found and acquired a vast number of official surveys of the shores and the uplands of Staten Island.

Through this wealth of accumulated and authoritative data, commencing with a survey of the shore fronts of Staten Island in the year 1728 and extending at intervals down to the present time, together with field-notes and field-maps of almost inestimable value, the American Title and Trust Company is able to locate and map the Crown Grant underlying any single building lot on Staten Island.

It may be thought by some that the English Crown did not in fact own Staten Island as a part of its private estate. They may even question Staten Island's vital connection with the Royal Manor of East Greenwich in the County of Kent, and may also insist that the Crown lands on Staten Island shall be treated as public Crown lands. They may urge that the character of the lands shall determine which were held as personal property of the Crown and which were held in trust for the people.

This is but a little longer route by which we will reach the same final conclusion as obtained by the shorter, more direct and correct theory of absolute private ownership by the English Crown of every square foot of land on Staten Island. This ownership includes uplands, meadows, marshes, streams, shorefronts and lands between high and low water mark and submerged lands to the very last limit and bounds of Richmond County.

Under such an incorrect theory of representative Crown ownership certain questions will naturally present themselves. What was then the character of the English Crown Grants as issued? What lands, if any, under such conditions could have been granted by the Crown in its own right, *as the actual owner thereof*, and what lands, if any, could have been granted by the Crown, the title to which it held in trust for the people?

Furthermore, the natural inquiry might arise as to whether there is any question or doubt as to the actual legal right and power of the Crown, when holding title to land in trust for the people, to grant the same to private individuals with or without the consent of the people fully and formally expressed?

In response to these very proper and pertinent questions, arising from a misconception of the complete title to and power over Staten Island lands vested in the Crown, the facts of history and the decisions of courts of proper jurisdiction completely meet the situation.

We have clearly and repeatedly stated that the English Crown held a perfect title to Staten Island by direct purchase, which fact legally settles once and for all the foregoing inquiries. Were that fact not established and if the basis of every title to lands on Staten Island depended upon the acquiescence of the people in any and all Grants thereof such objection is fully met upon examination of the original Grants made by the Crown to Staten Island lands. No Crown Grant to lands on Staten Island has ever been judicially voided and the people acquiesced in and recognized the binding force and effect of each such Sovereign Grant.

As a proposition of law lands are considered and designated real property without regard to whether the same are uplands or submerged. The fact of the presence of water upon the surface of a tract of land does not in any wise legally alter its character as land.

A Crown Grant to all the lands within the bounds and limits of a County covers all the soil within such County whether part of the same is lifted up in hills a hundred feet above sea-level or is sunk beneath the sea a hundred feet deep. In the eyes of the law, land is land regardless as to whether it carries on its surface soil, sand or sea. It is simply a question as to whether such land is included in the description contained in the deed and whether the Grantor has power to convey.

The waters themselves independent of the land and composing the seas, bays and navigable rivers are not the subject of private ownership. It has been judicially settled for generations that the sea, bays and navigable rivers are highways of commerce, free to the use of all citizens of the country having jurisdiction thereover. Commerce thereon may be regulated by and in the interest of the nation, but the sea itself, that is the waters thereof, can belong to no man as an individual proprietor.

It has been clearly determined that the Sovereign while *owning the lands under navigable waters,* as a part of the vacant and unappropriated lands of the realm, *can have no private ownership of the navigable waters* themselves. "The flow of water in the stream of a navigable river is in no sense private property." "Private right to running water in a great navigable stream is inconceivable." (Boviere Navigable Waters.)

The former rights of the Crown to the uplands of Staten Island as a part of the vacant and unappropriated lands of the realm was not and cannot now be successfully questioned. The facts thereof are too patent and the judicial decisions are too clear and conclusive to even admit of argument in relation thereto. Were it otherwise overwhelming confusion and chaos would exist in relation to the basis of substantially all titles not only on Staten Island but in all of our Eastern States.

Discussion has occasionally arisen in respect to the character of the title originally held by the English Crown to the lands between high and low water-mark on our Eastern tidal coast.

We may state the proposition as follows:

Man's domicil is on land, but he has an inherent natural right to navigate the seas. Public necessity, therefore, demands for him a right of approach to and egress from the waters of the Great Deep. To exercise that right he must traverse the shore between high and low water mark.

Were it otherwise the inhabitants of an island surrounded by tidal waters, would be practically imprisoned thereon because of the fact that surrounding the island there would be a narrow belt of land between high and low water mark owned by the Crown. To impinge the keel of a boat thereon would be to violate the territorial integrity of the land held by the crown.

Under such conditions the inhabitants of an island could only launch their boats or approach the shore at the moment of the high tides and then only in a boat of such shallow draft as to be almost unnavigable.

It has therefore been exaggeratingly claimed as one of the basic principles of human rights that the strip of land between high and low water mark belongs to the people. This rule does not apply to Crown lands or to land granted by the Crown. It is considered by some as communal land and is claimed to be similar to what was earlier herein described as the "Commons," the title being held in the Crown as trustee for the people. This theory is contrary to the governing decisions and especially untrue as to Staten Island.

A right of egress and ingress, however, is possessed by the people, but it must be and in the nature of things is a very restricted one. It is a right to go down to the sea in ships and to return therefrom. It was a right of "access to" and the right of "egress from" the waters of the Great Deep. No proprietor of said ribbon of land could take possession thereof so as to interfere with the ingress and egress rights of individuals. The theory of "No Man's Land, applying to such an important shore line, and when applied to any land is repugnant to law and contrary to good government, hence the title thereof was vested in the Crown as Chief Lord Proprietor.

The argument is at times advanced that the land between high and low water mark is neither upland nor submerged land. It has been contended that the Crown had no right whatever to make any grants thereof without the direct and fullest authority expressly given to it for such purpose by the people or by their duly authorized representatives. This peculiarly situated strip of land, under this theory, is compared by some to the "King's Highway," the title to which is in the Sovereign, but from which highway the public cannot be excluded or of which the public cannot be deprived by the Crown, excepting in case of great public need or danger, or the substitution of another highway therefor. A highway of travel and the right of ingress and egress are antipodal.

On the other hand, authorities have contended that the title to the land between high and low water mark, having been conceded by the people, to the Crown, it had a full and supreme right to make Grants thereof and that the grantees were under no obligation whatever to inquire into any arrangements or relations between the people and the Crown relating thereto. This may be consistently based upon the theory that "the King can do no wrong." That is, the people having conceded the title as being in the hands of the Crown to possess and control the strip of land between high and low water mark, as trustee for the people, then they were bound by the acts of their Sovereign. This presumption agrees with the Monarchical doctrine of "My Kingdom."

The above propositions have been at times advanced by parties who may have only superficially examined into the character and nature of the English Crown's title to and the English Crown Grants of lands on Staten Island.

In the earlier periods, or "middle ages," when the then sovereigns were given or acquired control of or title to *community* lands (we do not here refer to the Crown's title to "vacant and unappropriated lands") it was customary for the sovereigns to make Grants thereof either by Lease or otherwise. All such Grants of *communal lands* were then made, however, upon consultation by the sovereign with his Woden or wiseman.

In no instances were tidal lands held as communal lands. They were always held to be waste lands of the realm with the title thereto in the Crown.

In the combination of the Sovereign and the wiseman we have the crown representing itself and the Woden advising independently of the people. The wiseman was soon thereafter associated with other wisemen and they, when so combined, became the King's Council, selected and appointed *by the Sovereign, without consultation with or consent by the people.*

From this first and simple relation of Crown and Woden, there developed later on a limited monarchy composed of the Crown and the King's Council of wise-men, selected from and representing the people. Then Parliments followed on an elective basis with a voice in the Government but not as to Crown Grants in the American Colonies.

When civil government was organized in the English-American Colonies the English system of common law was transferred thereto and installed therein. The distance and time consumed in crossing the sea and also in the return voyage, were so great that the direct government of the Province of New York by the Crown and direct legislation over it by Parliament in England, were found to be not only inexpedient but absolutely impracticable.

Thereupon a Governor-General was appointed by the Crown for each American Province of Great Britain. These Governor-Generals were to represent and did represent the Crown itself and Councils were also appointed in the Province to advise the Governors.

Later on as the Province developed, a Colonial Assembly was established, which Assembly more fully and satisfactorily represented the people. In the earlier Colonial Period in America, because of the wide seas that separated the Colonies from the mother country, it was ordained by Parliament that any laws enacted by a Colonial Assembly and approved by the Governor-General of the Province should immediately have the full force and effect of an act passed by the English Parliament and approved by the Crown. It became operative forthwith upon its enactment. In the event, however, that such action did not meet with the approval of the Imperial Government at London, then the English Crown had the right to veto or annul such procedure and make void such act.

This right of veto was conditioned, however, only and absolutely upon the legality of all proceedings under the law during the lapse of time between the passage of the act by the Colonial Assembly with its approval by the Governor-General and the date upon which the official Crown veto reached the authorities in the Province where the law was enacted.

It was however the Council and not the Assembly which ratified the Crown Grant, to protect the Crown. It was done by the Crown's appointees and not by the people's representatives.

This statement is here fully made in order to show that any Grants which may have been properly made by the Governor-General of the Province of New York in behalf of the English Crown and which Grants were approved by the Council in New York, conveyed to such grantees the rights specified therein.

The people had no voice in the premises. Every property and political right possessed by a settler in the Province was founded upon a Crown Grant and he had no other title or right in the Crown lands in the Province.

This forever estops any and all traversing of the right of the Governor-General and his Council to the making of the English Crown Grants so issued to lands on Staten Island and especially and particularly to those Grants relating to lands between high and low water mark on Staten Island, and also to lands under water, to the "bounds and limits of Richmond County."

The Crown's right to make such Grants has not been traversed in two centuries. The rights thereunder have been privately held and enjoyed while vast improvements rest now securely upon such rights fully exercised.

After the Crown had made about one hundred and fifty Grants of land on Staten Island, largely through the acts of the Governor-Generals and their Councils, the English Crown desired, for reasons fully set forth in "THE MAJOR AND THE QUEEN," to close out to Lancaster Symes all of its remaining titles to lands on Staten Island and within the bounds and limits of Richmond County.

In order that no question might ever arise as to the regularity of issue and validity of the Grant to Lancaster Symes it was issued and sealed by and in the name of Good Queen Anne and under her Royal Seal. By direct and Imperial order that Great and Good Queen caused here Royal Grant to be issued to Lancaster Symes, closing out to him and to his heirs and assigns forever, as of her Manor of East Greenwich in the County of Kent, all the lands then remaining vacant and unappropriated on Staten Island, within the bounds and limits of Richmond County, together with the rights of fishing, oystering and other privileges not necessary to relate herein but fully and clearly shown in the books of public records.

To this Grant was attached the Imperial or Royal Seal, carved in wood with the Royal Arms represented thereon.

The boundaries of Richmond County as shown upon any standard map issued by the State of New York or by the State of New Jersey, or in fact issued by any responsible firm of map publishers are within the bounds and limits of the English Crown Grant to Lancaster Symes as made by the Sovereign Queen Anne under the Imperial Seal. No other Staten Island Crown Grant was made in which the lands under water conveyed by it touched at every point the limits and bounds of the County of Richmond. No other Crown Grant of lands on Staten Island extended at any point to such bounds and limits.

This Grant was not only issued by the Queen but it was approved by the Imperial Council in England. It was approved and ratified by the Colonial Council and by the Governor-General in the Province of New York. Thereupon it was properly patented and recorded. It constituted the highest form of and was the most important Crown Grant of lands ever issued for lands on Staten Island. It was accepted and acted upon by the people during the entire subsequent Colonial period and has never been challenged.

Since the date of its issue to the present time, covering a period of over two centuries, every generation has exercised the rights of land ownership thereunder through sales, possessions and improvements thereon.

In all that period of time neither Federal, State nor City Government has in a single instance denied legality or regularity in the issue thereof. No citizen has denied the full force or effect of the said Grant, while multitudes have enjoyed its protection and benefits.

THE NEW WORLD

AND

CROWN GRANTS

At the close of the fifteenth century the maritime nations of Christendom were all ecclesiastically dominated by the Roman Pontiff and acknowledged him as the spiritual representative of God on earth.

The "known world" prior to the epochal discoveries made by Columbus, had been largely divided up among the so called Christian nations.

The waste, vacant and unappropriated lands in each realm, were universally recognized as the personal property of the respective sovereigns.

These rulers under the doctrine of the divine right of Kings and claiming to represent divine authority in political sovereignty, held title to all lands within their domains over which the Almighty alone held sway and which lands no human held by right of ownership.

Suddenly the great navigator Cristoforo Colombo opened a door on the sea's western horizon and a "new world" loomed up out of the great unknown, as a gift from God.

These newly discovered continents consisted entirely of vacant and unappropriated lands, for the heathen inhabitants thereof were adjudged to be pagans, who under the unchristian code of inter-national law then prevailing, had no right whatever to life, liberty or the pursuit of happiness and much less any title to lands which the conqueror felt bound to respect.

The title to the virgin lands of the New World was admittedly and undeniably in God, for over them as yet no alleged Christian monarch by a so-called divine right held sovereignty.

The Portuguese and Spanish mariners promptly reported their new discoveries to their respective Sovereigns and the latter hastened to renounce all claims thereto at the feet of the Holy See in Rome, each however seeking a Grant therefor from the Pontiff.

Under the doctrine that the Pope at Rome was the visible head of the Church of God on Earth, there fell to him under international law the control of these virgin lands the title to which was conceded to be in God.

It was consistent therefore with such a world accepted theory that on May 4th, 1493, Pope Alexander VI, just seven weeks after Columbus cast anchor in the harbor of Palos, issued his famous Bull dividing between Spain and Portugal the newly discovered world.

The Papal Grant which was at that time issued to the King of Spain (Castile and Leon) on the one hand and the King of Portugal on the other, recited that it was "given with the liberality of Apostolic grace." Also that,

> "we at our own motion and not at your solici-
> "tation, nor upon petition presented to us upon
> "this subject, by other persons in your name,

"but of our pure free will and certain knowl-
"edge, by the authority of God Omnipotent
"granted to us through blessed Peter and of the
"vicarship of Jesus Christ, which we exercise
"upon earth, by the tenor of these presents
"given, concede and assign forever to you and
"to the Kings of Castile and Leon your succes-
"sors, all the islands and main lands discovered
"and which may hereafter be discovered, to-
"wards the West and South, with all other
"dominions, cities, castles, palaces and towns
"and with all their rights, jurisdictions and
"appurtenances, * * * ."

This Bull, of Pope Alexander VI, of which the foregoing is but an extract, "did shape the destinies of both hemispheres for centuries, leaving vast traces even to-day." "It practically gave a monopoly of most of the World's seas to Spain and Portugal and for a century thereafter the ships of all nations but these voyaged at their peril in the South Atlantic, Indian and Pacific Oceans."

Spain's Empire in South America, in Mexico, California and Florida rested upon it. Portugal's sovereignty over Brazil was under it and the title to the Philippines which the United States of America purchased from Spain eminated from it.

Strange analogies run between the original Grant made by Pope Alexander VI covering the New World and the Grant made by the English Crown to Lancaster Symes and others, referred to herein (Chapter 13).

The Pope alleges that his right to convey is *"by the authority of God."*

The English Crown says that its authority is *"by the grace of God."*

The Pope says that his Grant is issued by him *"of Apostolic Grace."*

While the English Crown Grant claims to be issued of *"Especial Grace,"* for said the religious authorities, "Ordination (of the Crown) is a sacrament and confers a special grace, which is permanent."

The Pope further records that he grants by his *"own motion,"*

The English Crown Grant represents being isued by *"meer motion."*

The Pope says that he makes the Grant of *"our pure free will,"*

And the English Crown Grant says *"we being willing."*

The Pope declares that he issues his Grant having *"certain knowledge."*

The English Crown likewise claimed *"certain knowledge,"* or correct and sure information.

In both Pontifical and English Crown Grants "lands" and "islands" are granted but with no specific reference to lands under water.

In no civilized country nor in any Court is it held that submerged lands were not included in the first great and original Grant issued by the Pope covering the virgin titles of the New World. On the contrary, every nation claiming thereunder maintained its title to submerged lands, under tidal waters, according to the universally accepted law of nations.

The Pope's original American Grant was made to the *Kings* of Spain and Portugal and *not to those kingdoms.*

The Grants made by the English Crown to its Grantees in America were in conformity with the same principle, *made by the Kings and not by the Kingdom.*

It should be remembered that the English claims of Divine right as to kingship and Crown land titles in America are, in theory, drawn from the same eternal source as claimed by Pope Alexander VI; that is, direct from God and *free from any intermediary ownership by a subject.*

The Anglican Church has direct descent from the Catholic Church at Rome.

Pope Alexander VI occupied the pontifical chair prior to the scism between Rome and London. The English Crown therefore claimed its right by divine authority manifest in the Church and under the solemn benediction of the Bishop of the Church of God bestowed at the coronation of the Kings.

If a written instrument is to be construed according to the intent of those who draw and execute it, then the English Crown Grants to lands in America are to be interpreted in the spirit of the royal minds issuing them.

The English Crown recognized that it had received its rights in the New World from God Almighty, whether the discovery was made by the Cabots or Columbus.

It then sought in carefully worded written instruments to convey to its Grantees unimpaired those sacred and solemn rights of property and privilege which it had received in its own solemn relation as a Divinely appointed and ordained Monarch.

In harmony with such a concept, Lancaster Symes, upon his receipt of the Crown Grant issued to him by Queen Anne, "the good Queen of England," covering lands on Staten Island and as an act of Fealty and Service to the Great Head and original Source of all titles, immediately endowed St. Andrew's Church at Richmond, Staten Island, the benefits of which endowment that church has enjoyed unto this day.

He conveyed to it two large tracts of the same lands granted to him by the Crown, one tract for a church and burial site and another tract for glebe uses.

The doctrine involving the sacred rights of property under Crown Grants harks back to the solitudes of God and is prophetic of a world's restitution to its Divine Proprietor, when the last man shall sleep amidst its final silences.

ENGLISH COMMON LAW

AND

CROWN GRANTS

In Colonial days English Comon Law recognized the issue of English Crown Land Grants as a monarchical prerogative entirely apart from the people.

We, in these more modern days and in this republic, look at English Crown Grants from the view point of democracy or of the dominance of the people.

The view point shifted for us in 1776. At that time the people seized the Crown of Sovereignty and absorbed all Crown rights. Justice requires that we shall not color our present thinking with the prejudice born of our larger liberties, when we consider the basis of certain Grants of land made by the Crown to private owners and which land should in our judgment, have been retained by the Crown for the use of the public at large. Such self-interest will not justify the seizure and forfeiture of private property rights previously obtained from the Crown, if so obtained in strict conformity with the Common Law at that time prevailing with its full approval and support of both Sovereign and people.

We should, in imagination, turn back the wheels of human progress and think out our mental problems of Crown Land Grant investigation in the dimmer, but correct and wholesome light of old English Common Law.

To properly interpret the language used in the English Crown Land Grants which were issued during the Colonial Period and which conveyed lands in the American Colonies, we must read them in the light of their times, and translate them in accord with the intent of the original Grantor and Grantee.

We must interpret such Crown Grants with proper regard for the then exact legal meaning of the words used therein and as at that time understood by the Crown and its English speaking subjects.

The language of a people changes as time progresses, but property rights acquired do not in the slightest degree alter under a languages shifting meaning.

Such changes are not limited to the style of chirography or to variations in the spelling of words, all of which are but trivial tokens of the deep and restless pulsations of mind waves, in the ceaseless tide of thought bearing words. Words may grow, expand and deepen under the vitalizing influences of human progress, or they may wither and shrivel from non use and become obsolete, with its benumbing and deadening effect.

Words in their evolution of meaning are flexible and absorbent. They take on new shades of thought, while lexographers show us that by their use in some connections they change their import in popular definition.

Legal definitions also take on new lights and shades as generations pass. He who would voice to us in modern language the thought of the past, or who would cloak the thought of the present in the phraseology of by-gone-days, must tread softly and feel his way with care and discernment along the pathway of human thinking. Otherwise his dictum will be inconsistent with the intent and expression of former thinkers and if followed may become subversive of the sacred rights of the present and future generations. Justice would not falsify the past to the injury of the innocent in order to forfeit merited properties and privileges and to destroy vested rights.

To us, many an old English word has lost from its bosom some rich gem of human emotion. Other words, through the polishing friction of use, under changing conditions, have taken on a new brilliance and luster.

In many of the old English Crown Grants we find that rich and grand old English word, "grace" inscribed therein.

That word was formerly full and fragrant with a meaning which expressed a wealth of unselfish love to one beloved and for love's sake.

To-day, the word, "grace," in common parlance, practically represents symmetry and the artistic in form, carriage and poise, or it may suggest a suave condescension.

Modern grace may be betokened by the handsome and stately feminine form and figure, while the old English word grace found its portrayal in the divine mental and spiritual endowments of the highest and noblest types of true and perfect womanhood.

Modern grace may be exemplified in death, but the grace of our forefathers was immortal. It never dies.

We Americans with somewhat less of ceremony

than brusqueness denied the "divine right of kings," at the same time we accord to our judiciary "the divine right of final judgment" affecting human relations.

To these our appointed dispensers of supreme justice, ancient English Crown Grants are brought for adjudication.

These Grants written in the language of the past and under the English Common law are to be interpreted in the language of the present day, with the sacred rights of vested property depending upon the faithful and correct translation and interpretation thereof.

Prior to the American Revolutionary war the Common Law of England, in so far as it could be adapted to the western continent became the basic law of the American Colonies. It became fundamental in America.

It underlaid the whole superstructure of American Colonial Institutions.

In pursuance of English Common Law the Colonies were developed. Under it the Governments therein were established, human liberties were therein guaranteed, and property rights were therein safeguarded.

Colonial institutions of almost every kind and nature existed by virtue of Royal Grants from the Crown, back of which was the old Common Law of England.

Under Crown Grants great commercial and trading companies were organized in America. The English Crown was the source of Granted Charters for the

Educational institutions and Ecclesiastical bodies founded in the Colonies.

Crown Grants were the source of Colonial land titles.

It is very clear that the existance of Colonial institutions, the preservation of human liberties in the Colonies and the protection of the rights of private property in the Provinces, all depended absolutely upon the integrity, inviolability and validity of the English Crown Grants which rested upon and acquired their force and effect from and under old English Common Law.

The Crown Grants so issued, by their terms, gave in unequivocal language certain valuable rights and properties in exchange for certain revenues or Quit-Rents as the consideration therefor.

The Crown under English Common Law had possessed the rights and properties so parted with and in return for such conveyances the Sovereign received the consideration provided to be paid under the terms of the Grants.

It was a fundamental proposition of law at that time as it also is now, that where two parties entered into contract relations for a valuable consideration, one of the parties thereto parting with the subject matter of the contract and the other thereto faithfully paying the agreed consideration therefore, and mentioned therein, the contract so made is irrevocably binding upon both parties thereto, unless voided by the free and voluntary consent of each.

It was true that fraud might void a contract, but not where the Crown was a party thereto. "The King cannot deceive" and "the King cannot be deceived" were maxims of law then well understood and accepted by King and people. How then could the issue of fraud be raised?

The people of the realm were fully and completely bound by the Royal Grants covering rights and properties in the Colonies and also in England.

Crown Grants were "open letters" or letters patent. They were not secret instruments but designedly and by established rule and practice issued in full sight of and with the knowledge of the public. Blackstone and other authorities tell us of the great care, precaution and painstaking publicity with which they were considered, prepared and issued.

The custom pursued by the successive Sovereigns in England, in this legal procedure with the full knowledge and tacit consent of the people, cannot now be successfully traversed on the theory that the King had no right to grant certain classes of land which he is alleged to have held in trust for the people.

Such Grants, if they had been made by the State in these days of democracy might with a color of credulity be so called in question.

In effect our statuary enactments restraining public officials from making Land Grants under certain conditions, not prescribed in Colonial days, in themselves admit that such practices were consistent with the common law and usage and can only be now restrained by statuatory enactments.

The argument based upon any theory of lack of Kingly power, if made, will not be sustained under our leading decisions. No such attitude was tenable under old English Common Law. It is to be said to the lasting credit of the New York Judiciary that the Courts of the State of New York have never voided an English Crown Grant. England had no constitution. The Magna Charta did not limit the right of the King to make Grants of land in America. "Such is undeniably the doctrine upheld in the State of New York." (Court of Appeals of State of New York.)

The English Courts had for generations prior to the American Revolt fully and completely recognized the English Crown's right to make such Grants throughout the realm. Simultaneously with the issue of Royal Grants in the Colonies the English Crown freely and unrestrainedly issued multitudes of similar grants in England, Scotland, Ireland and Wales.

The American Colonists accepted such Colonial Grant in good faith and paid their Quit-Rents. They then proceeded to lay thereon the foundations of an old civilization in a new world and under the protection of English Common Law.

All this was done with the full knowledge and consent by and of the English people. It was in harmony with the latter's free, frequent and contemporaneous indulgence and participation in like practices and policy exercised toward them by the Crown in both England and America. What was sauce for the English goose, was a sauce for the American gander.

"The English Crown looked upon America "as but the extension of the soil of England."

What was legally and morally right to an Englishman in England, was likewise legally and morally right to him when he migrated to the Colonies. There was no double standard of justice and equity, under English Common Law.

This statement is so fully made herein, in order to emphasize the fact that the English Crown Grants were no emergency inventions on the part of the Crown to meet conditions suddenly arising in consequence of the discovery and settlement of America.

The English Crown had been making Crown Grants for centuries prior to the discovery of the New World. The Grants made in America comprise but a chapter in the record of England's historic policy and practice.

Suddenly a new English ministry facing a deficit created by vast European War Expenditures, sought to increase the Royal revenues by imposing a tax upon the American Colonists not prescribed in their Grants and demanded increased revenues from the American Colonies.

The British Government undertook to "read into the Crown Grants" already issued, the right to abrogate, rescind, limit or amend the same without the consent of the Grantees.

It undertook to deprive Connecticut of its previously granted Charter and Plymouth Colony of its privileges. It attempted to enforce the same policy in other directions in America.

Yale College (1763) and other great commercial bodies vigorously protested against such attempted invasion of the rights enjoyed by them under Crown Grants.

The Colonists asserted and pleaded the sacred rights of contract and the inviolability of personal and public rights which had been granted to and acquired by them under the Seal of their Sovereigns.

The Crown had made the Grants and the Colonists had invoked the accepted rule of Old English Common Law that "the King can do no wrong." They claimed that the Crown did right when it issued the Grants to them and it could not rescind the Grants for that would be a legal and moral wrong. According to English thought, this was logic and not sophistry.

The Colonists flatly denied the Sovereign's right to demand by taxation any increase in revenues from those who held their properties and rights under well defined and clearly drawn Crown Grants, in which Grants their Quit-Rents were fully specified and their rights were clearly defined.

> "Staten Island is comprehended in the West
> "Riding of Long Island but payeth noe tax, be-
> "ing enjoyned by their patents to pay a bushall
> "of good wheate for each lott consisting of 80
> "acres."
>
> (Report Commissioner John Lewin to Duke of York.)

Taxation, then, without their consent would have been a flagrant violation of their granted rights and an arbitrary exercise of kingly power.

On this issue was fought the battles of the American Revolution. For the Colonist to have admitted the right of the Crown to alter, amend or rescind its Colonial Grants would have been the admission that all of their property rights, commercial privileges and personal liberties were held by Royal suffrance and favor. This doctrine once admitted, then these privileges might have been withdrawn through Royal caprice and at the King's pleasure. Liberty could then have been replaced by servitude and property could have been displaced by poverty at the will and whim of their Sovereign.

The Colonists well knew that English Courts and other legal authorities had uniformly maintained that the most dangerous power to be surrendered back to a government was the right to confiscate private property without adequate compensation therefor.

"So great moreover is the regard of the law "for private property, that it will not authorize "the least violation of it; no not even for the "general good of the whole community. If a "new road, for instance, were to be made "through the ground of a private person, it "might perhaps be extensively beneficial to the "public; but the law permits no man, or set of "men, to do this without the consent of the "owner of the land.

"In vain may it be urged, that the good of the "individual ought to yield to that of the com- "munity; for it would be dangerous to allow "any private man, or even any public tribunal, to "be the judge of the common good, and to de- "cide whether it be expedient or no.

"Besides the public good is in nothing more "essentially interested, than in the protection of "every individual's private rights, as modelled "by the municipal law. In this and similar

"cases the legislature alone can and indeed fre-
"quently does, interpose and compel the indi-
"vidual to acquiesce.

"But how does it interpose and compel? Not
"by absolutely stripping the subject of his prop-
"erty in an arbitrary manner; but by giving him
"a full indemnification and equivalent for the
"injury thereby sustained."

(Blackstone, Book 1, Chap. 1, p. 139).

All the above questions and more set the Colonists
aflame and civil war ensued. The Colonial Grants
were resealed in the blood of the patriot and ratified
and confirmed by victory.

The issue referred to was eternally settled in
America by the final decree of that Court of last resort, WAR. By that decision all English Crown
Land Grants became inviolate. "They mean what
they say, and they say what they mean." That decree
settled forever that nothing can be "read into them,"
or emasculated from them.

Crown Grants issued by the English Crown prior
to 1778 and covering lands in America were thereafter to stand, unquestioned, on any ground as to
their merits, and should be interpreted under English
Common Law with the full force and effect with
which they were issued by the Crown and received by
the Colonists.

In harmony with this final arbitrament of war, the
Governments of Great Britain and the United States
of America by solemn treaty stipulations, recognized, affirmed and confirmed the validity of the
Grants previously made by the English Crown.

The State of New York has likewise in each constitution adopted by it, solemnly ratified the English Crown Grants, which had been consumated in good faith and thereafter sustained through the horrors of a Civil War.

Hence the issued Crown Grants stand unimpeachable under treaty and constitutional provisions, as to the kingly power to issue the Grants or as to any trespass upon the rights of the people. *The people themselves denied this trespass by force of arms, compelled the Crown to ratify them and our Government affirmed that decision.*

Princes and People are alike bound by all treaties of peace made by their Sovereign Governments.

To reach a correct understanding of the rights and privileges conveyed under an English Crown Grant we should,

First   Disregard every statute enacted since such Grant was patented.

Second   Disregard every judicial decision made since the English Crown Grant in question was patented and relating to old English Crown Grants in general;

Excepting Only However

The legal definitions and interpretations contained in such decisions relating to the *Common Law of England existing at the date of the issue* of the Grant under consideration.

We must go back to the "stuffy little old English Court room" of the Colonial period. We must there consult the decisions of the old Court of the King's Bench, together with the opinions of other old authorities who then determined the rights and powers of both King and people, under old English Common law. At that time monarchical influences were in the ascendancy and democratic principles were in dormant embryo.

The accepted theory in those days was that all private title in and to lands came to the people through the condescension and benevolence of their Sovereign, who had received such title by divine right from God.

Therefore, according to that doctrine the title to all vacant and unappropriated lands in the realm *had never passed throught or from any member of the human family* and *no private rights* attached thereto or were inherent therein.

"Me und Gott" then as well as now (1918), proclaimed by the ruling Sovereign bespoke a theory of "close corporation," arrogated to itself by human Kingship; a complete monopoly of title by royalty in utter disregard of the comfort, happiness and welfare of the subjects in the realm. To dispute such a Royal right was considered treasonable to the King and blasphemous to God.

To all this the people assented and cried out, "Long live the King." Consequently a Crown Grant when made was accordingly naked and void of any reservations in behalf of the public, unless so expressed in the language of the Grant.

The old instruments of conveyance cannot at this late date be stretched to accommodate "the expanding rights of the people," however desirable that might be from the standpoint of public policy. Confiscation of private property without adequate compensation is subversive of good government, attacks the very foundations of human liberty, is contrary to the fundamentals of good law and defies conscience, for which perfidious proceedings our courts will not under any pretext or sophistry stand.

The only legal effect which the American Revolution had upon the titles to Crown lands in the American Colonies may be safely stated as follows:

> The Crown's absolute, undoubted and unassailable title to the *then vacant and unappropriated lands* in the Colonies was acquired by the people. Before the Revolution that title was in the Crown, in contradistinction from the people. They were "Crown Lands," utterly regardless as to whether they were uplands, lands between high and low water mark or submerged lands.
>
> The Crown could grant or lease to or withhold these lands from the citizens.
>
> When the American people by Revolution acquired these sovereign rights, the King's rights and the people's rights became *merged* in the State's title. As it now exists it is a perfect title, "as an incident of Soverignty", *but it does not affect the title to any lands previously granted by the Crown.*
>
> The tranfer took place when Democracy was enthroned in America.
>
> Such newly acquired popular rights were not retroactive. The Courts, both State and Fed-

eral, have settled that question for all time, as appears not only in uniform judicial decrees, but also in every constitution adopted by the State of New York, since its incorporation as a state.

Every English Crown Grant properly issued has been sustained by the Courts of New York when challenged.

Not one English Crown Grant has been voided by the Courts of New York.

ROYAL AUTHORITY

FOR

CROWN GRANTS

The English Crown took possession of Staten Island principally under two rights or claims of ownership. Its first claim was that by right of discovery, under which the English Crown asserted title thereto and had obtained political sovereignty and jurisdiction thereover. It maintained that upon taking possession of the Island it was but entering into lands to which it was fully entitled by right of prior discovery.

This was England's bold and defiant attitude when confronting the land grabbing nations of Continental Europe.

This doctrine, as originally promulgated by all of the powers of Europe and stripped of all sentiment and finesse, carried with it the cold blooded right to disregard the Indians as having any fixed abode, or any real title in the lands they occupied. They were decreed to be pagans, infidel dogs, objects for missionary effort and pious plunder. To enslave a pagan to a pious master was to put a bad thing to a good use. What shocking perversity!

England, however, in practice acted upon the more just and humane doctrine of purchasing from the Indians the lands in question.

Modern Christian sentiment does not tolerate such a pagan conception even though heretofore its taint may have dimmed the lustre of some of our court decisions.

Since the time of the conquest of England by William of Normandy, it has been maintained under English Common Law, that the titles to all lands in England must be traced back to an English Crown Grant, by either record or prescription.

> "He also that has a particular estate by
> "agreement of parties, must show, not only his
> "own conveyance, but the deeds paramount, for
> "there can be no title made to a thing lying in
> "agreement but by showing such agreement up
> "to the first original grant." (Introduction to
> the Law of England, relating to Real Property,
> Buler 1791 A. D., 6 Ed., p. 251.)

It appears to be implied by some authorities and in some decisions, that greater flexibility, latitude and scope should be accorded to a Crown Grant made to a municipality than to a private individual. In other words, it seems to be implied in some cases that a Crown Grant to an individual should be more strictly construed than should the same Grant when made to a municipality.

This theory did not exist under old English Common Law.

Such a dictum is seemingly inequitable, and has not appeared as a governing factor in any final New York decisions. If a sovereign state, with a population of ten millions (10,000,000) of citizens, by its properly constituted authorities, makes a Grant of a Bay or a Harbor to a municipality, where such a municipality has a population of ten thousand people, then nine million nine hundred and ninety thousand people are absolutely shorn of their title and interest in the land so granted, for the benefit of but ten thousand people. It is of no interest to the people so divested of title whether the same went to an aggregation or monopoly of ten thousand citizens, or to but one individual. The theory that such municipality holds such title as a trust for the people is "fine spun" in face of the fact that it holds it for the municipality to the exclusion and utter disregard of the citizens of the State at large. He who parts with a title or with all his interests in a title has little concern whether it be to a corporation in the form of a municipality or to an individual citizen, provided no further benefits accrue to him and he is divested of all rights therein.

In a Crown Grant of land where by its terms tidal water is fixed as a boundary thereof, high water mark is intended. This has been conclusively held and cannot be now questioned. If, however, such Royal Grant is one of political jurisdiction only then the boundary is to low water mark.

It has been further held, in the case of Baldwin vs. Brown (16 N. Y. 359) (and in 9 Johns 100) that natural boundaries are more to be regarded than artificial ones or those which are not permanent.

"By the Royal commission to Governors, the "Governor with the advice of the Council was "authorized to make Grants of the public lands "on such terms as might be deemed proper;

"which Grants, on being sealed with the
"Colonial Seal, and recorded, were to be
"effectual." (Town of Brookhaven vs. Strong,
60 N. Y., 56).

"It is well settled by authority that a State
"has the right to dispose of the unappropriated
"land within its own limits, and that *when a*
"grant has been made the title becomes vested,
"without any power in the State to rescind the
"grant, for fraud or otherwise, when the land
"granted has passed into the hands of the bona-
"fide purchaser for value, without notice."

"Nor unless fraudulent, can it be revoked at
"all, if its conditions are performed."

"Nor can a State constitutionally confirm a
"void patent, so as to divest a title legally ac-
"quired before the attempted confirmation."

(Girard on Titles to Real Estate.)

It is a fully established principle of international
law, well recognized by all legal authorities, that the
title to all vacant and unappropriated lands in the
realm is vested in the supreme sovereign. It has
been elsewhere explained herein, that in monarchical
countries such title rests in the Crown, while in democratic countries it vests in the chief Legislative body,
representing and voicing the mandates of the people.

"The Statute of Westminster, the Second to
"cover the case of persons claiming *common of*
"pasture by express Grant, seems to have been
"the foundation of the common law rule, that
"the absence of proof to the contrary, the soil

"of the Manorial Waste or Common is vested
"in the Lord." (History of English Law,
Jenks, 262.)

In fact, the doctrine is larger than this statement.
It is conceded that the title to all land was vested in
the Sovereign and that the ultimate title to all land
is now vested in the Sovereign, be it Crown or Legislature. It has become a legal maxim, "There is no
land without a Lord."

It has been to an extent and will be further herein
set forth that the Sovereign had and has power to
make Grants of any part or portions of the ungranted, vacant and unappropriated lands within the realm.
In certain circumstances a sovereign may make such
Grants with or without the authority of the people,
in accordance with the limitations and restrictions
with which the kingly power may be hedged about in
these days of constitutional or otherwise abridgement
of Kingly powers.

The original conception, and in fact the original
exercise of kingly power, was without let or hinderance. All modifications thereof and all constitutional
limitations placed thereon, have been extorted from
the Crown by the irresistible assertion of the right
of the people to supreme government in the affairs of
men.

An English Crown Grant to land in the English
realm carries with it precisely those rights and privileges accorded thereto by English Common Law prevailing *at the date of the issue thereof.*

In dealing with Staten Island titles to lands, no
question can be successfully raised as to the com-

plete and perfect regularity thereof. The Crown Grants from which all true titles on Staten Island must descend, bear the full authority of the English Crown, consented to by the Council, which authority was recognized by the people.

The absence therefrom of either the Royal consent or confirmation by the Colonial Council betokened an absolutely void Grant. Such authorization, however, by the Crown and Council renders such instruments complete and effective.

"Some, or at least one Grant has been made "without the advice of the Council, which is "conceived to be against the Queen's Commis- "sion or instructions." (Maladministration of affairs in New York, 1709.)

This shows that the Council's approval of Crown Grants *was by the Sovereign's "instructions" and not by any inherent right of any subject of the Crown to interfere in the matter.*

Fortunately all Grants made by the English Crown to land on Staten Island were made during a period of English History in which there was no increase or diminution of kingly authority, nor any variation whatever in the rights of the people in relation thereto. England has no constitution. Therefore, there were no constitutional changes, nor were there any variations in the English Common Law governing the rights of the Crown and the rights of the people in respect to these Colonial lands during the period covering their issue.

"From the passing of the Statute of Frauds
"in 1677, to the assembling of the first Re-
"formed parliament in 1832 we have, as has
"been previously pointed out, hardly a single
"statute of first class importance dealing with
"land law." (History of English Law, Jenks,
Page 236.)

The discussion, therefore, of such Grants as were
issued by the Crown becomes one of regularity in
procedure by the Grantor, compliance by the Grantee
and correct legal interpretation thereof. This study
can be proceeded with under the light of definite
knowledge, as to the Common Law of England at
that time prevailing, as set forth in the decisions of
her courts and the subsequent deliverances from the
American bench.

Foremost among these governing opinions are the
decisions of the Court of Appeals of the State of
New York. They are consistent, lucid and profound.

In speaking of the vacant and unappropriated lands
in the realm, Digby says in his History of the Law
of Real Property, "there remained a very large proportion of the land of the country lying waste and
uncultivated and used only for pasture of sheep and
cattle, for feeding swine on the acorns and beech
mast, or for supplying wood for building, repairs and
fuel. It was primarily regarded as the common stock
from which grants might be made."

Bede, in the eighth century, speaks of it as lands
which "ought to be granted to ecclesiastics or to
warriors."

Vacant and unappropriated land in early days

was sometimes designated "folk land." The title to the same was held by the Crown. Digby again says: "Besides grants of folkland, to be held as book land or as private property, it seems also to have been common to allow individuals temporary or possessory rights over folk land without altering its character as public lands. The reversion (to use a later expression) still remained in the community at large, or in the King as the representative of the community. There is evidence that in some cases various rents, dues or services, in money or time had to be rendered for the enjoyment of rights over folk land."

Bede, in speaking of these vacant and unappropriated lands said, *"When the country was brought under the government of a single King, this land seems to have been regarded as in an especial manner the property of the King,* and is frequently spoken of as *the King's* folk land."

He further states: "Besides *the grant of whole districts* of this land, to be held as 'Book land,' we frequently find that rights of pasture and other beneficial rights over it *are granted away to individuals by the King* in the usual form. There can be but little doubt that this unoccupied land came to be, more and more regarded as the land of the King—'Terra Regis.' Hence grew in later time the conception that all the land was originally vested in the Crown; that the King is prima facia owner of all the unoccupied land, *even of the shore of the sea below high water mark."*

In another reference thereto he says: "In early times these rights were probably regarded as rights of common or public lands which the King would share with others. *Later the property was looked upon as vested in the King.* The commoners having rights *in alieno solo.*"

> "If it be no longer known of whom the lands
> "are immediately holden; then the King, as
> "Great and Chief Lord, shall have them by
> "escheat: for to him fealty belongs and *of him*
> *"they are certainly holden by presumption of*
> *"law and without the necessity of proof."*
> (Cruise's Digest of the Laws of England respecting Real Property (1808) Vol. 2, title 30.)

At the close of the Revolutionary War, the Billop lands on Staten Island were escheated by the State of New York, on the ground that the then owner, (not the original) Christopher Billop, "had given aid and comfort to the common enemy."

Digby says, in his Law of Real Property, that if a grantee "incurred forfeiture for treason, the rights of the lessor would not be affected." In this case, however, the State of New York had stepped into the shoes of the English Crown and had become the ultimate owner of Billop's lands, subject only to any Grants therefrom.

> "A grant of land has been defined as a public
> "law standing on the statute books of the State
> "and is notice to every subsequent purchaser
> "under any conflicting sale made afterwards."
> (2 U. S. App. 581.)

A patent is conclusive against all whose rights commence subsequent to its date (7 Wheat,

212). It conveys the legal title and leaves the equities open. (15 Peters 93.)

A patent of land is the highest evidence of title and is conclusive as against the government and all claiming under junior patents or title until set aside or annulled, unless it is absolutely void on its face. (2 Wall 525; 23 Howard 235; 104 U. S. 635.)

When the State has once made a valid grant to lands to one party, it cannot afterwards reconvey the same lands to a different person. (Van Home vs. Torrance, 2 Dall, 304 to 320.)

It has been held that these provisions, by implication, confirm all patents and Grants of land by the Crown prior to October 4th, 1775. (People vs. Clarke, 10, Barb. 120, Affirmed in New York, 349.)

Property rights acquired before the American Revolution were also protected by provisions in the treaties of 1783 and 1794, between United States and Great Britain. Article 6 of the United States Constitution provides that all treaties made, or which shall be made under the authority of the United States shall be the Supreme Law of the land.

The Federal Courts, therefore, have jurisdiction in cases involving English Crown Grants, which are protected by international treaties.

The Thirty Sixth section of the Constitution of 1777 (New York State), declares that nothing therein contained shall be construed to affect any Grants of land made by the authority of the King, prior to the 14th day of October, 1775.

In the case of the People vs. Clark (9 N. Y. 349) the Court of Appeals of New York declared,

> "the learned Justice of the Supreme Court, "whose able opinion in this case we are review- "ing, a most respectable authority upon ques- "tions of titles to lands depending upon ancient "grants, has declared that *this provision of the* "*Constitution has always been regarded as con-* "*firming the Royal patents granted before the* "*Revolution.*"

In the work entitled, "Two Centuries Growth of American Law, by Members of the Faculty of the Yale Law School," the statement is made that,

> "Before the Revolution the People had ac- "customed themselves to the assertion that their "charters had made them certain irrevocable "Grants, one of which was that they were to "possess all the rights and privileges of Eng- "lishmen."

The authors of that work further state, "An executed grant is inviolable, because it is a contract. The party who made it has lost certain rights. The party who received and accepted it has acquired them; and each must stand by his bargain."

"President Clap, in 1763, had set up successfully a similar claim as to the Charter of Yale College, when the General Assembly was threatening to amend it without the consent of the Corporation." (Dartmouth College vs. Woodward 4 Wheat, 518.)

"The laws which subsist at the time and making of the contract, and where it is to be performed enter into and form a part of it, as if they were expressly referred to, or incorporated in its terms." (White vs. Hart U. B. 13, Wall 646.)

The fundamental idea underlying the titles to lands in the United States is that the State, "if one of the old Thirteen," is seized of all the lands within her limits *not granted;* and as to the new States and Territories the seizen is in the United States to the like extent. (Clements vs. Anderson, 46 Miss. 581.)

On the Independence of New York, the *ungranted* Crown lands vested in the State and continued to be granted by letters patent under the Great Seal. (N. Y. C. RR. Co. vs. Brockway Brick Company, 158 N. Y. 470.)

In New York, when by the Revolution the Colonies became separated from the Crown of Great Britain and a Republican Government was formed, the people succeeded the King in the ownership of lands within the State, *which had not already been granted away;* and the people thenceforth became the source of all private titles.

> People vs. Trinity Church, 22 N. Y. 44.
> Jackson vs. Hart, 12 Johns (N. Y. 77).
> Wendell vs. People, 8 Wend. (N. Y. 183).

But with respect to land that before October 14th, 1775, *had been legally granted to individuals* by the Crown, or to which the title *had been legally acquired by individuals* in any other way, neither the Revolution nor the change in the form of Government, *nor the declaration of the Sovereignty of the People worked any change of forfeiture in the ownership of such property."* (Gerard on Title to Real Estate.)

The Grant made by the English Crown to the Duke of York became vested in the English Sovereign when the Duke of York became King of England. The right of the King of Great Britain to make this Grant to the Duke of York, with all its prerogatives and powers of government, cannot at this day be questioned. "The rivers, bays and arms of the sea and all prerogative rights within the limits of the charter undoubtedly passed to the Duke of York, and were intended to pass, except those saved in the letters patent. The words used evidently show this intention." (By Chief Justice, Martin vs. Waddell, 16 Peters 367.)

> The Grants to the Duke of York contain:
> "Together with all the lands, island, soils, riv-
> "ers, harbors, mines, minerals, quarries, woods,
> "marshes, waters, lakes, fishings, hawking, hunt-
> "ing and fowlings."

It will be observed that this description is even more restricted than the language in the Symes Staten Island Grant, to wit,

> "Together with all and singular the woods, un-
> "derwoods, trees, timber, feedings, meadows,
> "marshes, swamps, pools, ponds, waters, water
> "courses, rivers, rivuletts, runs and streams of
> "waters, brooks, fishing, fowling, hunting,
> "hawking, mines and minerals, standing, grow-
> "ing, lying or being or to be had, used or en-
> "joyed within the bounds and limits aforesaid;
> "and all other profits, benefits, advantages,
> "hereditaments and appurtenances whatsoever.

"unto the said pieces and parcels of land and
"premises, belonging or in any way appertain-
"ing (except and always reserved out of this
"our present Grant all gold and silver mines)."

The language of the Grant to Lancaster Symes
carries with it all fullness, as far as the same could
be applied to the vacant and unappropriated lands
on Staten Island and to all vacant and unappropriated
lands above and below water within the bounds and
limits of Richmond County covering all of the rights
received by the Duke of York under the original
Grant to him.

> In the case of Martin vs. Waddell (16 Peters,
> 367) the Supreme Court of the United States
> held, "According to the theory of the British
> "Constitution, *all vacant lands are vested in the*
> *"Crown,* as representing the nation, *and ex-*
> *"clusive power to grant them is admitted to re-*
> *"side in the Crown,* as a branch of the royal
> "prerogative. It has been clearly shown that
> "this principle was as *fully recognized in Amer-*
> *"ica* as in the Island of Great Britain."

The Dutch were completely divested of all lands
claimed by the English under the Cabot discovery,
and such title became revested in the English Crown.
(Fowler's Real Property Law, 2nd Edition, Chap. 1,
Title 2.) This issue was settled in accordance with
a treaty made between England and Holland. The
Staten Island Indians had always protested that
deeds made by them to the Dutch had been obtained

by fraud, and that the true consideration and proper compensation had never been paid to them by the Dutch.

There was no change in tenure under Crown Grants in consequence of the passing of the statute of *quia empores* (18 Ed. 1; Delancey vs. Piepgras, N. Y. Rep.).

> "The power now possessed by the Govern-
> "ment of the United States, to grant lands, re-
> "sided, while we were Colonies, *in the Crown or*
> *"its Grantees. The validity of the title given by*
> *"either has never been questioned in our Courts.*
> "It has been exercised uniformly over territory
> "in possession of the Indians.   *   *   *   All
> "our institutions recognize *the absolute title of*
> *"the Crown,* subject only to the Indian right of
> "occupancy, and recognize the absolute title of
> "the Crown to extinguish that right."   (Will-
> iam B. Hornblower, 14 Amer. Bar. Assn. Rept.
> 264, 265.)

THE INDIAN

AND

CROWN GRANTS.

It is a fully recognized fact of history that when the early European settlers landed upon the shores of Staten Island they then found it in full and complete possession of the American Indians. The Indians held undisputed sway over its villages, hunting and fishing grounds, and stood prepared and ready at any time to defend the same, as was clearly shown in their subsequent deeds of valor when resisting the unjust and offensive encroachments of the early settlers.

Authorities have somewhat disagreed as to the precise nature of the title held by the American Indians to the soil which they possessed. The continental chancellories of Europe, promptly upon the discovery of America, promulgated their decrees branding the American Indians as nomads. They laid down the proposition of international law that the European Government had an absolute right to each and every land on the American continents, which either they or their representative citizens should discover.

Proprietorship by right of discovery was asserted, with utter disregard to what were the true and inalienable rights of the American Indians.

Modern historic research has disclosed the fact

that the aborigines of America had their established and accepted forms of government; that the various tribes well understood and recognized the territorial bounds and limits of their respective domains.

> "That it is a difficult matter to discover the "true owner of any lands among the Indians is "a gross error, which must arise from ignorance "of the matter or from a cause which does not "require explanation.
>
> "Each nation is perfectly well acquainted with "its exact original bounds; the same is again "divided into due proportions for each tribe and "afterwards subdivided into shares to each fam-"ily, with all which they are most particularly "acquainted. Neither do they ever infringe "upon one another or invade their neighbors' "hunting grounds." (Sir William Johnson to the Lords of Trade, 1764 A. D.)

In some cases single tribes were independent, self-reliant, and maintained their sovereignty and the integrity of their soil against all comers. In other cases a powerful confederation was formed by treaty between a group of tribes. In other instances weaker tribes came by special treaty under the protection of more powerful neighbors.

To a large extent, peace and happiness prevailed among the tribes, each respecting the rights of the other in and to its own hunting and fishing grounds. Any invasion of these indispensable sources of food supply was always met by prompt defense and swift and fierce retribution.

A sharp distinction should be drawn between the attitude of the English Government towards the Indians and the general practice of the Colonists towards the natives.

The European settlers promptly appropriated the Indian's food supply from sea and land. The great pressure of a new advancing civilization forced the coastal tribes back upon the neighboring interior tribes, in utter disregard of tribal boundaries. Antagonism and conflict immediately developed between the natives, superinduced by the white man's overthrow of the Indian's political, economic and tribal relations.

Tribes, evicted from the lands which they had inherited from their forefathers, were driven by hunger to pirate upon the hunting and fishing grounds of other tribes which had heretofore been their friends. The latter, unable to spare food from their naturally sparse and limited supply, arose in arms and fought their former friendly neighbors.

This invasion by the white race upon the Indian civilization developed a period of intertribal wars that brought to the surface the fiercest elements in the Indian nature. These wars continued until the tribes became almost extinct or were driven far from their native soil.

The Indian first fought the white man in defense of his own land, villages and food supply; then the various Indian tribes fought among themselves, as exiles and wanderers struggling together for an insufficient food supply.

It is well understood that a majority of the first settlers were adventurers, pirates and freebooters of the sea. In many cases they were criminals, exiled from home, or were wild and dissipated sailors who were prepared to venture anything, and to commit almost any crime in order to repair their broken fortunes. The "Mayflower" and other ships with their precious cargoes of religious and freedom-loving exiles were like doves amidst the hawkes and vultures of the sea.

Information from the early Colonies passed slowly to the mother countries. Vivid and distorted accounts were given of the attitude of the natives and the acts of the settlers. The first impressions formed in England and on the continent of Europe regarding the aborigines were that they composed roving and cruel bands, better classed among the wild animals of the forest than to be considered a part of the human family.

Impressions formed and conclusions arrived at by European authorities based upon such erroneous information developed the doctrine which became woven into international law, that the American Indians were nomads or wanderers; that they were pagans and had no real vested or true title to the soil they occupied, and that they were unworthy of or in fact did not possess any real national life or substantial political existence.

History, however, shows that the English Government soon became better advised, and that the States General of Holland recognized to a degree the injustice of this dictum of the white civilization as pronounced against the red man.

Thoughtful historians and learned legal authorities have conceded that the Indians had somewhat more than a possessory right to the lands they occupied and have admitted that they had an inherent right in and to the title to the soil they occupied. The title so belonging to them, however, was vested in the tribe at large and not in the individual Indian. Justice gained a few points in the historic and judicial triumph for the Indian over the doctrine of nomadship; but even to this day, as appears in one of the decisions of the Supreme Court of the United States, the impression still prevails in many authoritative quarters, false though it be, that the Indian had only a general possessory right to their lands. (Johnson vs. McIntosh 8 Wheat O. M., Rep. 543.)

In the above mentioned decision, emanating from the most profound and dignified judicial body in the world, the Court says, "The potentates of the Old World found no difficulty in convincing themselves that they made ample compensation to the inhabitants of the New by bestowing upon them civilization and Christianity in exchange for unlimited independence."

The fact remains that, in a deed made and executed by and between the Dutch and the Staten Island Indians for the sale by the latter to the former of Staten Island, the Dutch fully recognized *a complete title to the Island as vested in the Indians* and as having descended to them *from their forefathers.*

Later on, when the Staten Island Indians sold Staten Island to the Duke of York, the Dutch deed having proved abortive, *the English fully recognized the title to the soil as being vested in the Indians* and as having been derived by them *from their ancestors.*

These two instruments, both quasi-official, representing two European powers, *in effect committed the civilized world* to the doctrine that the Staten Island Indians were the *"true and lawful owners"* of the Island, as having descended to them as a heritage from time immemorial.

Neither party to an executed and fulfilled contract, under which both parties have received and approved the benefits thereof, is in a legal position to deny its premises.

In the drafting of the foregoing deed, which in fact conveyed to the English the villages, together with the hunting and fishing grounds of the Staten Island Indians, neither party thereto deemed it essential that the said deed should set forth in detailed description the conveyance thereunder of uplands, beach, shore and lands under water.

The English Crown well understood that under English common law the presence of water on any portion of lands conveyed need not be set forth in the instrument of conveyance.

The Indians fully realized, as did the English, that the conveyance of Staten Island to the English Crown carried with it the Indian's hunting and fishing grounds as well as the latter's unfailing source of food supply, the natural oyster beds connected therewith.

Staten Island historians, as well as many of the patriarchs of the villages in Richmond County, tell us that over against many of the old sites of the Indian villages on Staten Island were to be found until recent times enormous mounds of oyster shells that had required the industry of many generations to accumulate.

Modern etymology has opened up the secret of the Indian languages, and lo! it is found that their rivers, bays, seas and lands possessed names with descriptive meanings, which names had become traditional among the descending generations and were well and fully understood by their tribes.

These names now properly interpreted are conclusive proof that the Indians occupied fixed habitations, generation after generation, "for a period of time wherein the memory of their oldest men ran not to the contrary."

At the present time we find a pathetic remnant of the Shinnecock Indians living upon the site of one of their ancient Long Island villages.   From time immemorial down to the present they have maintained their right in and to a portion of Shinnecock Bay.   In those waters, without failure for centuries, they have planted and grown the almost unequalled Shinnecock oysters and clams.

It is an interesting fact, and worthy of note, that in many respects the Indian common law was strangely analogous to the English common law.

The Indian well understood that he was the owner of the beach, with all that the same implied.   Hence, we find a certificate given on January 15th, 1662, by the Shinnecock Indians living on Long Island, to one Captain Topping.   In this certificate they acknowledge the conveyance of a certain beach to him.

The Indians did not in anywise limit their titles to the beach.   This we discover in an Indian deed to a shore front in King's County, New York.   The deed was dated May 13th, 1664.   The conveyance was for "both of upland and marshes anyway belonging

thereto." We find also, in the same deed of conveyance, "beach or beaches, as namely that running out
more westerly." In addition thereto we read, *"with
the island adjoining* and is at the same time by the
ocean sea wholly enclosed." It is well to consider the
legal force and effect of the words "with" and "adjoining" as used by the Indians.

We have in the foregoing deed by the Indians a
conveyance of upland, beaches "with the island adjoining" thereto. All these were in close proximity
and extending to and under tidal water. This deed
made no reference to "riparian rights" or "lands below high water mark," or "submerged lands." The
language was different, but equally clear and inclusive.

The Indian, as under English common law, deeded
his land and did not consider water on the land as
property to be included in a deed or mentioned in the
description thereof.

That the Indians' and the English Crown's views
as to deeds of conveyance for an island coincided
most harmoniously is happily illustrated in the case of
Gardiner's Island, in Suffolk County, New York.

On May 3rd, 1639, the Indians executed a deed of
conveyance thereto to Lyon Gardiner. The latter
took possession thereof. The Gardiner family has,
ever since that date, maintained possession thereof
through the lineal descendants of the original grantee.
They have held against the world a well recognized
and perfect title to uplands, the land between high
and low water mark, and the land extending out into
and under the great deep below low water mark.

We find, however, in the colonial records that the

English Crown also made a grant to the said Gardiner, conveying under the grant the same island without any detailed description contained therein covering uplands, beach and shore with the submerged lands.

The Province of New York joined in this same Grant by the Crown to Lyon Gardiner. Both the English Crown and the Province of New York have always recognized the full and complete title of the said Gardiner in the beach, shores and the land below low water mark.

After the Revolutionary War, and the incorporation of the State of New York, the policy of the State towards Gardiner's Island was and still is in complete harmony with the policy of the old Indian, the English Crown and the Province of New York. It has never asserted or claimed any shore front rights about Gardiner's Island.

On the other hand, the Gardiner family has never tolerated any trespass thereon by private citizen or body politic.

The rights granted to Lyon Gardiner and the rights granted to Lancaster Symes, by the English Crown, the Province of New York and the State of New York "are on all fours" with each other, excepting only, however, that from a legal viewpoint the description of lands conveyed under the Symes Grant is far more comprehensive than in the Grant to Gardiner.

The narrow constructionist might imply from this statement relating to Gardiner's Island that possibly the Indian's part in the transaction was but a sale of the upland, they quitting the Island with no particular thought as to the lands under water.

Such a conclusion is but a misapprehension and misconception of the Indians' claim and right of title.

On March 14th, 1648, the Indians made a deed of a certain tract of land to Theophilus Eaton and Stephen Goodyear. The deed covered a tract of land at what was known as Acquabauck, Long Island. The deed recites *"together with the land* and meadow *lying in the other side* of the water southward.

Here is a deed given by the Indians for land on both sides of and *in the waterway,* or stream. The English and the American common law both admit that the Indians must have owned from each shore to the center or thread of the stream. The tribe held proprietorship below low water mark. The doctrine of christendom is that "there is no land without a Lord."

Unless we strip the poor Indian of the commonest rights accorded to the meanest citizen in England or America under similar circumstances, this latter conveyance by the Indians was a proper exercise of the rights of proprietorship, as the waters of the stream were tidal waters and involved every class of land from upland to submerged land below low water mark. Most assuredly both parties to the transaction so understood it and acted upon it.

To make clear, however, that the Indians really understood what the term submerged lands meant, when making deeds, the Massachusetts colonial records disclose *a deed* made by the native Indians in which the name used, "Aupauk," in itself, when translated, means, *"the flooded or overflowed land."*

The Indian's clear, clean and comprehensive knowledge of his rights to lands under water are also disclosed in an agreement bearing date 1665, which reads as follows:

"The bounds agreed upon between the Shinnecock and the Unchechauke Indians before the Governor Nicoll are, "That the Shinnecock bounds to the westward are to Apaucock Creek. That the Unchechauke bounds to the east are Apaucock Creek; that the middle of the river is the utmost bounds to each, but that either nation may cut flaggs for their use on either side of the river without molestacon or breach of the Limetts agreed!" (Book of Deeds, Vol. II, p. 125, Office of Secretary of State, Albany, N. Y.)

This agreement clearly shows that two neighboring Indian tribes claimed and each recognized in the other title to lands under water. The agreement also contains a reciprocity clause that would have done credit to the Hon. James G. Blaine or to the Hon. John Hay.

In the year 1667 the inhabitants of South Hampton, in New York Province, brought an action against the inhabitants of Southold in the New York Provincial Court of Assize to determine the boundary between the two towns based upon the purchase of lands from the different Indian tribes. A witness by the name of Edmund Shaw testified that the Chief of the Montauk Indians had shown him that one tribe owned the land to high water mark on the opposite side of the river, and to prove it took him to the opposite bank and showed him a tree marked by the Indians. Two Indians were called to rebut that testimony. They testified that each of the two tribes on the opposite sides of the river owned to the center or thread of the stream. To prove this they related how a dead bear was found floating in the stream and its carcass was divided between the two tribes, one tribe taking the flesh and the other tribe the skin and the grease. The Court decided that each tribe's title extended to the middle of the stream. This was a tidal river.

Important and incontrovertible evidence is at hand revealing the fact that the Indians held proprietorship to their fishing grounds on the Atlantic Coast as an absolutely necessary and vital source of food supply and that it was their custom to resort thereto in time of famine as well as in time of plenty.

We quote from a letter written by Roger Williams to Governor Vane in 1637: "The Pequots are scarce of provision and therefore (*as usual,* so now especially) they are in some numbers come down to the seaside (and to islands by name Munnawtawkit and Manattuwond especially) to take sturgeon and other fish, as also to make new fields of corn in case the English should destroy their fields at home."

It is a well-known fact that the early settlers found the Indian with his fishing weirs established in the tidal streams. The Colonists quickly imitated him in this practice, and in instances secured Grants for the establishment of the same, by them, in navigable waters. We have in point Governor Andrus's Grant made in 1676 to John Cooper, giving to the latter the right to establish fishing weirs in two tidal streams on Long Island.

In order to throw additional light on this subject, it may be stated that there were many places along the Atlantic Coast referred to and described in deeds by the Indians, which, when interpreted, mean "fishing places." As fishing is not for the uplands, it is fair and logical to presume that such places so referred to in deeds made by the Indians comprehended lands under water.

The wardship thrown about the American Indians by the English Government in Colonial times was not an impairment or in derogation of the proprietorship rights of the American Indians, either tribal or as individuals.

So keen was the commercial instinct in the white race and so innocent and unsophisticated were the American Indians in the matter of bargain and sale, that had the English Government not thrown about the Indian tribes its paternalistic protection in the matter of the title to their villages, fishing and hunting grounds, the deceit and treachery of many of the early settlers would have precipitated many additional frontier conflicts.

Pursuant to such benign policy, the English Government, when having political jurisdiction over lands owned and possessed by the Indians, would not permit the native tribes to sell their lands to the settlers without the sanction of the Crown. Apparently this power asserted by the English Government was never used arbitrarily against the natives.

It was not in essence the denial of a title in and to the right on the part of the Indian to sell the land in question. It was but a regulation under the police power pertaining to political sovereignty and solely exercised for the protection of the natives against unscrupulous traders.

Until the year 1871 the policy of the Federal Government of the United States was strictly correct in its professed attitude toward the respective Indian tribes as independent sovereignties. It conceded to them the right of treaty with the United States Government upon terms of national equality. Many treaties were made between the Federal Government and the respective tribes, in reference to lands owned by the Indians, as well as matters of trade and other relations.

International law does not admit wandering tribes and roving bands into the sisterhood of nations. Where great Sovereign powers, like the Federal Government of the United States enters into treaty relations with political organizations on a plane of equality and mutual respect, it is in itself an admission of nationality, which carries with it not only independent political sovereignty but fixed habitation on lands of independent proprietorship.

It is true that the Federal Government prohibited the Indian tribes in the United States from making or entering into treaties with political powers other than the Federal Government. This had nothing to do with the sovereignty or proprietorship rights of the Indians, excepting only that the necessity of defense of its national life compelled such an attitude on the part of the Federal Government.

"Necessity is paramount to law."

RIPARIAN RIGHTS

AND

CROWN GRANTS

It is an interesting fact that when the Duke of York purchased Staten Island of the American Indians, the same became a part of the Crown's private Manor of East Greenwich in the County of Kent in England. It was to that manorial office that Queen Anne required ultimate accounting to be made, by her American representatives, of the quit-rents collected by them from this portion of her East Greenwich estate. In other words, the English Crown made leases to its subjects of properties in East Greenwich, England, connected with the estate there. Simultaneously and in like manner and form it made leases or grants to portions of the *same estate* on Staten Island. The Crown's tenure of land on Staten Island was the same as its tenure in East Greenwich, England.

As Staten Island was strictly manorial property of the English Crown, or at least property owned by the Crown through private purchase, the Island had in no wise a quasi-public character. All the lands above and below water and between high and low water mark on Staten Island were in the Crown's private proprietorship. The public had no right or title in the uplands, in the lands between high and low water mark, or in the lands beyond and below low water mark in the County of Richmond. The title to the entire Island was vested in the English Crown, without let or hindrance. Therefore the public did not then have, nor has the public since that time, ever had, by implication or otherwise, any right, title or interest, except by escheat or purchase, in any lands on Staten Island.

The State of New York inherited or succeeded to no title to any lands on Staten Island, hence its true and correct disavowment of any such ownership, as made by the office of the Secretary of State at Albany, the Land office and the State Surveyor and Engineer.

The doctrine of riparian rights, as commonly understood, does not apply and never has applied to Staten Island lands. It is indisputably true that each and every Grant made by the English Crown to lands, regardless of where or how situated, is limited to the express terms of the said Grant. Such a Grant cannot and never has been construed as implying, as against the Crown, any more rights and priviliges than clearly stated therein. The lesser title (the subjects title) can never presume as against the greater title (the Crown's title), unless the habendum to the Grant by proper qualifications shifts such presumption, as it does in the Grant to Lancaster Symes covering lands on Staten Island.

Judge Mason, in the case of Furman vs. the Mayor of New York (Superior Court 1851), In passing upon a question of a claim by riparian owners to rights against the Crown covering lands below high water mark, brushed it aside by stating:

"There cannot be two owners to the same
"piece of land, under the conditions set forth."

He further added:

"If the owner has the estate in fee it follows
"that it can be granted. There is no such quali-
"fication in the books that the soil be granted to
"any person but the riparian proprietor."

Lord Hale quoted two leading decisions (De Por-
tubus P. 13) in which it was held that *the riparian
proprietors, owners of the upland or river bank, had
no legal claim as against the King to any land below
high water mark.*

In other words, the owner of the bank of a tidal
stream or navigable water had under English Common Law, no legal claim to what we now term to be
"riparian rights" as against the Crown title to lands
below high water mark.

"No reason suggests itself why the defend-
"ants should have a higher right against the
"Grantees of the King than they would have
"held against the Sovereign of Great Britain,
"had he continued the owner of the soil."

(Trustee of Town of Brookhaven vs. Smith,
188, N. Y., 74.)

This doctrine is uniformly held by our courts. The
riparian rights are recent and *statutory* and relate to
lands *not previously granted and now owned by the*
State.

"Gore was the owner of the uplands adjoin-
"ing the lands under water embraced in the

"Grant. The ownership of the adjacent up-
"lands, however, gave him no title to or interest
"in the lands under water in front of his prem-
"ises. The titles to lands under water within
"the realm of England were by common law
"deemed to be vested in the King as a public
"trust, to subserve and protect the public right
"to use them as common highways for com-
"merce, trade and intercourse."

"The King by virtue of his proprietary inter-
"est could grant the soil so that it should be-
"come private property, but his grant was sub-
"ject to the paramount right of public use of
"navigable waters, which he could neither de-
"stroy nor abridge."
(People vs. The Staten Island Ferry Co.,
68 N. Y. 71.)

The use of navigable waters for commercial purposes and the title to the land under such waters are
an entirely separate and different proposition.

Upon the termination of monarchical sovereignty
in New York, the State acquired all of the rights of
the English Crown in and to lands wherever situated *but subject, nevertheless to any and all rights
previously granted by the English Crown.* The
Grants so made by the English Crown prior to the
American Revolution were guaranteed by the American Government in its treaties with Great Britain and
are also guaranteed by the various constitutions
adopted by the State of New York.

Therefore, neither the Federal Government at
Washington, nor the State Government at Albany,

nor the City Government of Greater New York, nor the people at large have any right, title or interest in or to any lands properly granted to private parties by the English Crown, regardless of whether such lands are above or below water, or between high and low water mark.

The present theory of riparian rights, as held in the popular mind, developed largely from the habit of the people sailing upon the sea to find at all times and under all conditions a harbor, a haven of refuge, or a landing on the shore without let, hindrance or trespass. It also arose from the theory that the land owner on the shore was the only one excepting the King, who could protect the same against those who would otherwise trespass and take possession of land under water immediately adjacent to his upland on shore. He could best guard the shores against poachers, pirates and smugglers. He could shoot his arrows, throw his lances, or discharge his firearms from his shore at an enemy seeking to land or to anchor his boat near the beach.

"The right of jurisdiction and the right of "property must not be confounded." (Delancy vs. Piepgras.)

This riparian right of jurisdiction recognized as pertaining to land between high and low water mark and in favor of the littoral proprietor was secondary or subservient to the King's title to all lands under the tidal seas and was exercised by a servant of the Crown.

The Freedom of navigation is admitted. The use of the waters for commercial purposes is recognized, but on the contrary New York has penalized trespass upon lands granted under tidal waters.

The Crown might have delegated jurisdiction to the owner of the upland for military purposes, that the latter might aid his sovereign in defense of the sea. The littoral owner might have stood guard over the shore for his sovereign, against hostile trespass by the King's enemies. "The King maintained possession of the lands under the great deep through his mighty navy." The King's subjects settled along the shore and sustained a watch for him over the landing places where the tide ebbed and flowed, but this loyal attitude gave such subjects no implied right to confiscate from the Crown the lands so guarded by them.

The same principle was adopted by the world powers in according political sovereignty to a nation over what is known as the "three mile shore limit." At the time of the adoption of this principle the utmost reach of the cannon effectively used by the nations was a distance not exceeding three miles from the shore.

Exponents of international law are now agitating the extension of this limit to 20 miles, in consequence of the greater range of modern guns.

In the Act settling the boundary between New York and New Jersey, enacted by the Legislature of the State of New York on February 5, 1834, in Article V, Sec. 2 it is provided that,

"The State of New York shall have the ex-"clusive jurisdiction over the wharves, docks and "improvements made and to be made *on the*

> "*shore of Staten Island* and of and over all ves-
> "sels aground *on said shore*, or fastened to any
> "such wharf or dock, except that the said ves-
> "sels shall be subject to quarantine or health
> "laws and laws relating to passengers of the
> "State of New Jersey which now exist or may
> "hereafter be passed."

Here we have an express declaration on the part
of the Legislature of the State of New York that
Staten Island has "shores." There can be no distor-
tion of language or straining of the true intent of the
words used when we say that the *Legislature stands
committed of record that such shores belong to Staten
Island.* It further recognizes that certain *wharves,
docks and improvements* have been made and are to
be made *on said shores*, etc. Neither the Federal
nor the State Courts differ as to the fact that "the
shore is that piece or tract of land between high and
low water mark."

No citations are necessary to support this
thoroughly known and understood proposition of
law.

The legal conclusion has, however, been summar-
ized as follows:

> "The shore is that space of land on the bor-
> "der of the sea which is alternately covered and
> "left dry by the rising and falling of the tide,
> "or in other words, the space between high and
> "low water mark."
>
> (Amer. & Eng. Encyl. of Law "Shore.")
>
> "The State having granted in fee a strip of
> "land under water extending from high water

"mark cannot thereafter give another the right
"to erect a public dock thereon."
   (DeLancey vs. Wellbrock, 113 Fed. 103.)

The argument as to the non-ownership by either
the City of New York or the State of New York
in and to any land on Staten Island between high
and low water mark is a simple and plain one. The
Indians owned the title in fee to Staten Island. This
was admitted by Holland and England in deeds
drawn by them with the Staten Island Indians, which
deeds were ratified, confirmed and are matters of
public record. These deeds admitted the descent of
title in all lands on Staten Island to the Indians, and
that such descent was by inheritance from their forefathers. Thereupon the English took title and possession of all lands on Staten Island by purchase from
the Indian owners.

Later the English made Grants of certain lands on
Staten Island and then made a final and inclusive
Grant to Lancaster Symes covering all the vacant and
unappropriated lands on Staten Island within the
bounds and limits of Richmond County.

The State of New York, for a valuable cash consideration subsequently confirmed and ratified the
title in Lancaster Symes. It recognizes, as all
authorities do, that all waters about Staten Island including the Fresh Kills are tidal waters. The Legislature admits that Staten Island has a "shore." It
is very trite to say that the shore is land between
high and low water mark, is on the Island and a
part of it.

Nearly all Staten Island Grants were limited to high water mark.

The Crown Grant to Ellis Duxbury (March 19th, 1691) and the second Crown Grant to Ellis Duxbury (August 26th, 1708) both include and Grant to him a shore front of great extent and value, "to low water mark thence by low water mark rounding as it runs."

If the English Crown could and did properly and legally grant miles of land on Staten Island between high and low water mark, it is conclusive proof that land between high and low water mark on Staten Island was a part of the Crown's estate. When the Crown granted to Lancaster Symes (October 27th, 1708) all of its unappropriated lands, he unquestionably obtained title to the then ungranted lands between high and low water mark.

The final grant to Lancaster Symes covered and included all vacant and unappropriated lands on Staten Island to "the bounds and limits of Richmond County."

The human mind is helpless in any attempt to conceive any theory upon which these admittedly "vacant and unappropriated lands," between high and low water mark, constituting the "shore" of Staten Island, can possibly be excluded from the scope of the Grant made by Queen Anne to Lancaster Symes.

The Courts hold that when the State has once made a valid grant of lands to one party it cannot afterwards reconvey the same lands to a different person.

Under *modern statuatory enactments* the Courts consistently hold that,

> "A grant by the State of New York of land
> "under water between high and low water mark
> "is absolutely void if made to any other than
> "to the owner of the upland adjacent thereto."

(The Champ. & St. Law. R. R. Co. vs. Valentine Barb. 19, 484.)

As a corollary thereto, Courts are bound to and do decree that any Grant made by the State of New York to lands under water, *which lands had been previously granted by the Crown, is void.*

The United States Federal decisions are very clear on this point.

> "A statute which purports to convey only
> "such right of title as the State may have, be it
> "valid or invalid, is not unconstitutional as im-
> "pairing the contract or vested rights of persons
> "holding under valid, prior independent titles."

(Devine vs. Los Angeles, 202 U. S. 313, 335.)

It has been held that,

> "The doctrine that private property shall not
> "be taken without due process of law, nor with-
> "out compensation being made therefor applies
> "to private property devoted to public use.
> "Confiscation without compensation is repug-
> "nant to the due processes and equal protec-
> "tion clauses of the 14th Amendment in the
> "United States Constitution."

The Court has also by decree duly warned the public that,

> "Where money is voluntarily paid to a re-
> "ceiver of the land office after a party's atten-
> "tion has been called to a legal risk attending
> "such an act, the payment must be regarded as
> "made in mistake of law and not in mistake of
> "fact and an action will not lie to recover it
> "back." (Encyl. of the U. S. Supreme Court
> Reports "Public Lands.")

> "When the land between high and low water
> "mark has been granted to another, the upland
> "proprietor has no right to land below low
> "water mark." (Sage vs. the Mayor of New
> York, 154 N. Y. 154.)

At the present time it is and for many years it has been unlawful in the State of New York for the Land Office to issue any grant to land between high and low water mark, excepting to the owner of the uplands. This is, however, *by special enactment.* "It was not always thus." It was not so in Colonial days, during which period every Staten Island Grant was made.

It has been very pertinently held that "a right to the soil is very different and distinct from a mere right to have the first offer when the owner is obliged to sell. Yet even the latter is inconsistent with the entire power over a perfect, absolute estate in fee."

In the case, however, of (Beach vs. the Mayor) the Grant of land under water made by the State of New York, to one Ward and others, jointly, covering lands about Ward's Island in the East River, the Court held such Grant valid. This was so held, notwithstanding the fact that there were certain upland owners who were not included among the Grantees. The Court took the same position in the case involving the Grant made by the State of New York to land under water about City Island, where other upland owners were not included among the Grantees.

These two Grants *were made by the State prior to the enactment of the present statute* prohibiting Grants of riparian rights to parties other than upland proprietors.

> "The owner of land bordering on high water
> "mark on the tide waters of the State who has
> "not obtained the State titles to the lands lying
> "in front of his property and below high water
> "mark, has no power to charge the latter with
> "any easement which will be forceful against a
> "subsequent grant by the State of its title on
> "those lands."
>
> (Atlantic City vs. New And Pier Co. 63 N.
> J. 644.)
>
> "The Andros patent, dated September 29th,
> "1677, includes the lands between high and low
> "water mark and substantially all of the waters
> "of Oyster Bay Harbor."
>
> (Condert vs. Underhill, 167 App. Div.
> 335.)
>
> "Under the Common Law as it existed in
> "1693 a littoral proprietor had no right to main-

"tain a wharf or other structure on land between "high and low water mark."

(Trustees Town of Brookhaven vs. Smith, 188 N. Y. 74.)

(Reversed on other grounds but this principle held.)

"The mere fact that in the 19th century the "Crown was a mere trustee for the benefit of "the public should not be utilized to deprive "individuals of rights which they had acquired "from it at a time when it had unquestioned "authority to grant the right." (Water and Water Rights, Farnham, Vol. 1, P. 191.)

It certainly had the right to make such Grant in the 18th century from its personal Crown estate.

PUBLIC BATHING PLACES

AND

CROWN GRANTS

The English Common Law doctrine that the people have the right to pass to and fro between high and low water mark on tidal and navigable water is part of the outgrowth of the humanitarian principle that inhabitants of uplands have an inalienable right of exit from and ingress to the sea for commercial and fishing purposes, as well as for the privilege of travel.

Such egress and ingress are based upon the simple right of direct passage between upland and water. The people at the present time, however, seek to establish the right of passage at their will, and to meander to any distance along the shore between high and low water mark, thereby seeking to give to such strip of land the characteristics of a public highway. This claimed right on the part of the public appears to be coming into qualified favor with the Courts. In some cases it has been held that if admitted the said usage must be one of continuous passage, and not of delay, detention or obstruction.

The Courts clearly and consistently hold that this right pertains *exclusively to ungranted lands and never to lands previously granted.*

It is judicially settled that in no event can the public erect thereon any structure or in anywise conduct themselves in a manner that will interfere with the freest use thereof, by the sovereign owner. A Crown Grantee thereof has admittedly in himself the exclusive rights theretofore possessed by the Crown and people.

It is settled that the owner of the upland must not interfere with the free and unrestrained movement of the public along the strip of land between high and law water mark *if the same has not been previously granted.* Such use by the public is founded upon custom and usage and obtains while the title thereto remains vested in the Crown or State, but ceases when by Grant the shore becomes private property. Such use by the public, however, may be forbidden by the Crown.

This free and unlimited range of movement claimed by the public along the shores of navigable streams, but confined and restricted between high and low water mark had a unique genesis. It was founded upon a custom based upon a commercial necessity, but which custom is now extinct.

In the earlier days of English navigation, vessels that sailed the high seas of commerce and which found their motive power in wind and canvass and not in the galley slave, impressed seamen, or steam, were somewhat unwieldy in narrow waters and were difficult to navigate on small winding English rivers. Frequently these commercial vessels appeared at the mouth of a navigable stream and sought to steer their way to commercial towns and villages, situated thereon at a distance in from the sea. At times it became necessary to tow these vessels, by horse power, to such interior ports or destinations.

Under primitive conditions now prevailing in present day Alaska, we find packs of Eskimo dogs dashing along the shores of its rapid streams and towing the native canoes, against the swift currents of the rivers. No one, however, has presumed to assert the claim that this practice dedicated those shores to pleasure strolling and other public uses in defiance of Government Grants.

The right of free passage along the shore of English streams, between high and low water mark, for the horses used in towing the vessels to their ultimate landing places was contended for by navigators in early days under the plea of commercial necessity.

This claim so made by the mariners, was contested by the land owners. The necessity of the seamen was the basis of a plea which was challenged from the view point of injury to the owners of the uplands. The right was judicially accorded as a temporary privilege in some cases and refused in others. On occasions the Courts permitted the necessitous trespass on one shore of a stream while it denied the right on the opposite shore of the same stream. In certain cases the mariners were allowed by the English Courts to travel a distance along one shore, then compelled to halt their vessels and transfer their teams to the opposite bank, such transfer causing considerable loss of time, expense and labor, to the master of the ship. This was ordered done that the least possible injury from trespass, should occur upon land situated on the banks of the stream. In one case, decided by the King's bench, it was observed that such passage along certain banks of the Thames River, between the sea and London on which vast and valuable estates had been developed, was not to be entertained by the Court. The Court would not permit substantial injury to the proprietors of the shore.

In that instance, to have permitted such passage along the shore above high water mark would have greatly injured cultivated lands, improved lawns and beautiful gardens. Such travel along the Thames below low water mark was impracticable while the land between high and low water mark along the river was then Crown land. In general, however, the land between high and low water mark, was not adapted for agricultural purposes nor for any cultivatable use.

This ribbon of land between high and low water mark was owned by the Crown. Burden bearing animals in case of necessity could travel it, without making it a public highway. Humans, in case of need, could traverse it, though its sands were wet and its soil heavy. It was not adapted for a public highway for travel, excepting under the pressure of a special and peculiar emergency.

No flight of imagination in those practical times pictured it as a pleasure promenade. It was the propelling power of a great need and not the allurements of pleasure that gave force and effect to the doctrine of temporary use, by the public, of a strip of land, the title to which was vested in the Crown. From this state of facts was developed, in part, the theory that the land between high and low water mark was held by the Crown in some peculiar way in trust for the people.

In no event could such temporary use constitute a restraint or bar upon any improvements thereof by the Crown or its Grantee, which improvements, when made, would make such use impossible.

English Courts denied to the public the right to trespass thereon for pleasure purposes, and in cases even held as trespassers those who claimed and appropriated it for bathing uses, and even held that pushing a baby carriage on a beach constituted a trespass upon private rights.

Public travel thereon was a right developed from a commercial necessity which is now obsolete and rested upon a custom long since terminated. However, some Courts in their decisions and counsel in their pleadings appear to lean toward and favor this as a present inherent public right. The ancient commercial but restricted access to and egress from the sea, by those who were domiciled upon the uplands and who desired to sail the deep was conceded and provided for but cannot now be successfully demanded by the public for beach loitering, sea bathing and board walk strolling.

Rights that have emanated from and rest upon customs that have subsequently become obsolete are deemed at law to have become in themselves, void. "Necessity makes that lawful, which otherwise is unlawful." (10 Co. 61) When necessity ceases, such rights created thereby and founded thereon automatically terminate.

It has been shown that the so called "right of the public" to move along the shore of navigable waters is based upon an obsolete commercial necessity, which in the past could only be exercised by the public when and where that commercial necessity existed. "Reason is the soul of law, the reason of the law being changed the law is also changed." (Leg. Max.)

The public could exercise the right on Crown lands below high water mark, but only so as not to interfere with or trespass on the rights of the true owner of the uplands above that mark. It was impracticable for the public to exercise such right of travel below low water mark. It was, however, by Royal clemency and favor that the public use of such Crown land was permitted and not by inherent right of the people thereto. The many Crown Grants of Ferry privileges, in the Province of New York, and especially on the Hudson River show the arbitrary exercise of Royal authority over shore fronts and beaches, giving exclusive rights by Grants thereto excluding the public therefrom in utter disregard of the upland owners. These Grants covered in instances many miles of shore fronting many upland owners and in total disregard thereof.

This exercise of authority by the Crown was without any confirmation by the Provincial Assembly, it being well understood and admitted that it was an indisputable prerogative of the Crown. The present ferry between Newburg and Fishkill-on-the-Hudson is operated under such a Royal Grant.

The English Courts denied to the public the right of free passage along the Crown's shore front where commercial needs did not exist. Nothing could be erected by the public upon this strip of land, nor could any obstruction be placed upon it by the public in the exercise of any such limited and exceptional rights as hereinbefore described.

The King had the right to condemn such obstructions if erected, as perprestures, and to seize and destroy the same or he might retain and operate the same as his own property, provided they did not interfere with the public rights of commerce on the sea.

Hence the King's Bench sustained the validity of the Crown Grants to shore fronts and the punishment of those attempting to use without a Grant the land between high and low water mark for bathing purposes. The very nature and character of this exceptional and temporary right of passage along the shore between high and low water mark explains its intent.

"The intent of the lawmakers is the essence "of the law."   (Lex. Max.)

The right of the public to use the foreshore in England, was and is, very restricted, as is shown in the following decisions:

"The public's common law right with respect "to the sea, independently of usage, are rights "upon the water not upon the land; of passage "and fishing on the sea and on the sea shore, "when covered with water, and although as "incident thereto, the public must have the means "of getting to and upon the water for those pur- "poses, yet it appears that by and from such "places only as necessity or usage have approp- "riated to those places, and not a general right of "lading or unlading, landing or embarking "where they pleased upon the seashore or the

"land adjoining thereto except in case of peril
"or necessity."

(Blundell vs. Catterall 5B and Ald, 268.)
Lord's Court of England.

"In this country the right of the public to use
"the foreshore *when not granted* in fee is much
"more liberal."

(State of New York, Steeple Chase Co., N.
Y., July 11th, 1916.)

"The English case of Blundell vs. Catterall
"(5B and Ald 268) settled that there was no
"common right of bathing in front of a shore,
"where the shore the *locus in quo had been*
"*actually granted* to the Lord of the Manor.
"Justice Holrayd states this to be the question."

(Estates and Rights of the Corp. N. Y.,
B. 111.)

The pleasure seeking public may not exercise a
right that overrides private vested interests, where
they demand for pleasure a privilege extended under
the pressure of a commercial necessity. They cannot
expand the doctrine of necessitous public use of
Crown land, accorded by Royal clemency and favor,
into a right to trespass upon private land along a
pathway that by no inference or implication can be
presumed to be "a highway of pleasure."

The strand of land above high water mark is the
bank on and in which it is admitted the public has no
common right. The shore or beach is the narrow
strip of land between high and low water mark which
is always, excepting for the moment of ebb tide, par-

tially or entirely flooded. It is always wet, disagreeable, and liable to be overflowed by the surf, disqualifying it for pleasure purposes, unless artificially reclaimed. This reclamation may only be done by the Crown, or by the State, or, if such shore has been previously granted then by such grantee.

With the removal of the original commercial necessity for the exercise of the right of travel along the shore by a limited portion of the public on exceptional occasions, the demand by the general public for the exercise of the same right, "when on pleasure bent," is untenable.

In brief, the rights claimed at the present time by the people to the land between high and low water mark may be explained as follows:

The Crown originally owned (a) ; the upland (b) the land between high and low water mark; and (c) the land below low water mark. It alone had power to grant any portion of the three mentioned classes of land. The Crown did frequently and unhesitatingly exercise such right.

When the King granted upland extending to tide water the Grant was limited to high water mark, unless by the language of the grant it specifically included land between high and low water mark or submerged lands. When by some great volcanic upheaval the level of the sea bottom changed and from large areas of submerged lands, water receded, then the ungranted land theretofore under water became upland, *the title thereto still remaining in the Sovereign.*

The right of the people, which were rights of commerce and travel *on the water,* then went to sea with the water. No special popular rights then adhered to or attached to the land so released from the water. It was Crown land whether submerged or upland and the people's rights pertained to the use of the water alone.

There were no mysterious popular rights adhering to the shore fronts, or to the lands under water. "Ignorance doth cloak our thoughts in Mystery and is the mother of ghosts and phantoms."

The popular right of access to the sea, "the highway of commerce," is substantially the same right which goes with the sale of a land-locked lot. A reasonable and proper way, lane or road must be provided by the Grantor to the Grantee, so that the owner of the land-locked plot of land may have ingress and egress between it and "the King's highway," or the public highway on land.

The owner of such a plot must accept and be satisfied with such a reasonable and proper route as may be designated by the surrounding property holders or holder. The two cases are parallel.

A gradual accretion or erosion of a shore front continuing imperceptibly through a period of years, likewise shifts with it the title to the land between high and low water mark. This is not true, however, when a sudden, violent and radical change occurs. In the latter event the boundaries are readily determined and easily marked.

In the case of Staten Island, *every Crown Grant* now legally accepted *was approved by the Crown and* the Council. Staten Island passed completely into or under private ownerships, "to the bounds and limits of Richmond County." The Grants issued by the Crown and failing of confirmation by the Council are admittedly void. The Crown represented imperialism, the Council consisted of the Crown's advisors. The Crown consented to each Grant subject to its approval by its appointed council.

When the final Grant of land on Staten Island was made to Lancaster Symes in 1708, *not one square foot in Richmond County remained vested in the English Crown.* Consequently the State of New York upon its organization did not succeed to the ownership of any land thereon. Hence the candid admission by the State of New York (in 1873) that the State was not the owner of any land on Staten Island.

> "So great, moreover, is the regard of the law
> "for private property, that it will not authorize
> "the least violation of it; no, not even for the
> "general good of the whole community.
>
> "If a new road for instance were to be made
> "through the grounds of a private person, it
> "might perhaps be extensively beneficial to the
> "public; but the law permits no man, or set of
> "men, to do this without the consent of the
> "owner of the land.

"In vain may it be urged that the good of the "individual ought to yield to that of the com- "munity; for it would be dangerous to allow "any private man or even any public tribunal to "be the judge of the common good, and to "decide whether it be expedient or no.

"Besides, the public good is in nothing more "essentially interested than in the protection of "every individual's private rights, as modelled "by the municipal law. In this and similar "cases the Legislature alone can and indeed fre- "quently does interpose and compel the indi- "vidual to acquiesce."

"But how does it interpose and compel? Not "by absolutely stripping the subject of his pro- "perty in an arbitrary manner; but by giving "him a full indemnification and equivalent for "the injury thereby sustained."   (Blackstone, Bk. 1, Chap. 1, p. 139.)

UNDER SEA LANDS

AND

CROWN GRANTS.

There can be no ambiguity or legal uncertainty as to what constituted originally the boundaries of Staten Island at the time the English Crown Grants were made to lands thereon.

We find in the Colonial Law of New York (Vol. I, 1664 to 1719) that on November 1st, 1683, the Colonial Assembly of the Province of New York passed "An act to divide this province and dependencies into shires and counties."

In that Act it was provided that "The County of Richmond to contain all of Staten Island, Shutters Island, and the Islands of Meadows on the west side thereof."

It should here be observed that what is now sometimes called "The Island of Meadows," situated at the mouth of Fresh Kills on Staten Island was not one of the "Islands of Meadows" referred to in the above statute. The present Island of Meadows was not an island, prior to the American Revolution, as is clearly shown on the official survey by the officers of the English Crown.

On October 1st, 1683, as shown in Volume I of New York Colonial Laws, the Colonial Assembly again passed an act providing that the County of

Richmond should contain all of Staten Island, Shutters Island and the Islands of Meadows on the west
side thereof.   In other words, Richmond County was
to include no more and no less than the above.

The Act *does not read* that Richmond County shall
be composed as aforesaid, *plus additional land belonging to the Crown of England, extending under
the water about Staten Island but not belonging
thereto.*   It distinctly and clearly states that the
County shall be composed of the Islands referred to.
Immediately upon the passage of the said Act the
boundaries of Staten Island were defined and
mapped, as is clearly shown on the early maps of the
County.   These boundaries appear in the records of
the contention between the State of New York and
the State of New Jersey over the boundaries between
the two States.   This contention was inherited by the
States from the Colonies of New York and New
Jersey.

The County of Richmond only acquired political
jurisdiction over and no proprietorship in the lands
referred to.   The statutes, however, together with
the Crown's Surveyor, clearly show what lands were
included in Staten Island.   This conclusion is in strict
harmony with the language of the final Grant to
Lancaster Symes, which included:

> "All the before menconed Pieces and parcells
> of vacant & unappropriated Land and Premises
> "and all and singular the Heriditaments and
> "appurtenances thereunto belonging within the
> "bounds and limitts above in these Presents
> "menconed and expressed together with all and

"singular, the woods, underwoods, trees, timber,
"ffeedings, meadows, mashes, swamps, pooles,
"ponds, waters, watercourses, rivers, rivulets,
"runs and streams of water, brooks, ffishing and
"ffowling, hunting, hawking, mines and miner-
"alls, standing, growing, lyeing, or being or to
"be had, used or enjoyed in them the bounds
"and limitts aforesaid and all other profitts,
"Benefitts, Advantages, Hereditaments and ap-
"purtenances whatsoever unto the sd pieces and
"parcells of lands and premises belonging or in
"anywise appurtyying except and always re-
"served out of this our present Grant all gold
"and silver Mines."

The Grant to Lancaster Symes was made after the
organization of Richmond County and its terms comprehended all the vacant and unappropriated land in
*the County of Richmond, which comprehends the
whole of Staten Island.*"
The above deduction, that Staten Island lands extended to the bounds and limits of Richmond County
is in full and complete accord with Blackstone's
authoritative statement:

"A stream or watercourse is considered as
"part of the land." (Blackstone.)
"For land," says Edward Coke, "compre-
"hendeth in its legal signification any ground,
"soil or earth whatsoever; as arable meadows,
"pastures, woods, moors, waters, marshes,
"furzes and heath; it legally includeth also all
"castles, houses and other buildings, for they

"consist," said he, "of two things: land which
"is the foundation and structure thereupon, so
"that if I convey the land or ground, the struc-
"ture or building passeth therewith. It is ob-
"servable that water is here mentioned as a spe-
"cies of land, which may seem a kind of sole-
"cism; but such is the language of the law; and
"therefore I cannot bring an action to recover
"possession of a pool or other piece of water, by
"the name of water only; either by calculating
"its capacity, as, for so many cubic yards; or by
"superficial measure, for 20 acres of water; or
"by general description, as for a pond, a water
"course, or a rivulet; but I must bring my action
"for the land that lies at the bottom and must
"call it 20 acres of land covered with water: for
"water is a movable, wandering thing, and must
"of necessity continue common by the law of
"nature, so that I can only have a temporary,
"transcient, usufructuary, property therein:
"wherefore, if a body of water run out of the
"pond into another man's, I have no right to
"reclaim it, but the land, which that water cov-
"ers, is permanent, fixed and immovable: and
"therefore in this way I may have a certain sub-
"stantial property of which the law will take
"notice and not of the other." (Blackstone,
Book 2, Chap. 2: 18.)

"From the earliest times in England, the law
"has vested the title to and control over the
"navigable waters therein in the Crown and Par-
"liament. A distinction was taken between the
"mere ownership of the soil under the water and

"the control over it for public purposes. The
"ownership of the soil is analogous to the own-
"ership of dry land and was regarded as *jus*
"*privatum* and was vested in the Crown; but the
"right to use and control both the land and the
"water was deemed a *jus publicum* and was
"vested in Parliament. The Crown could con-
"vey the land under water so as to give private
"rights therein, but the dominion and control
"over the waters in the interests of commerce
"and navigation for the benefit of all the sub-
"jects of the kingdom could be exercised only by
"Parliament." (Commonwealth vs. Alger 7
Cush. 53.) (People vs. N. Y. Staten Island
Ferry Co. 68 N. Y. 71.)

"As in England, the Crown and Parliament
"can, without limitation, convey land under pub-
"lic waters." (State of N. Y. vs. Steeplechase
Park Co., N. Y., July 11, 1916.)

In 1718, Lord Cornbury granted to the corporation of the City of New York,

"All that aforesaid vacant and unappropriated
"ground lying and being *on the said Nassau*
"*Island.*" (Pg. 161, England 162.)

This Grant was confirmed by the Montgomerie
Charter of 1730. The language of this conveyance
is significant as an illustration of the principle that
there is no distinction in fact to be drawn between
land covered by water and land above water. *The
grant of the whole bed of the East River for a con-*

siderable distance between the Manhattan and Brook-
lyn shores was made without once referring to the
land as being under water.

These grants have been upheld by the Courts.

As a legal proposition there is no difference between land under water and land under air.

The air is transitory. "We know not whence it
cometh or whither it goeth." It is on the land now,
but in a moment it has fled and other atmosphere
takes its place. No deed can bind it, no property
rights attach to it.

The water is migratory. The winds chase it, grav-
ity dominates it and the tides composed of water
sweep on in never ending restlessness. It is on the
land for a few moments of time, then away it flows,
while other and strange waters take its place, but only
for a hand breath of time, when they too give place
to other floods.

Birds fly in the air and fish swim in the sea. Boats
navigate the one while airplanes navigate the other.
The hydro-airplane sails on them both.

Docks extend out into the one while dwellings and
skyscrapers pierce the other.

The laws of navigation govern them both. The
State dictates the length and construction of the docks
while at the same time it has full power to limit the
heighth of the buildings on land and the construction
thereof.

The public may sail the seas and navigate the air
though the land owner holds title to the land under
both. This is pursuant to the public's right of travel
and commerce.

The land under each is fixed, stationary, and is the

object of proprietorship. The elements represented in the water and the air cannot be.

Hence the law ignores both air and water in legalizing a transfer of land and looks to land alone as the object of proprietorship.

> "A grant of land described by metes and "bounds carries with it lands under water within "the bounds." (Condert vs. Underhill, 95 N. Y. S. 134, 107; App. Div. 335.)

Therefore, Colonial Legislators did not err when they declared that Sand Bay was "*on* Staten Island," and again when they declared that it was "*on* the easter most part of Staten Island." Not East of, but "*on* Staten Island."

The final Crown Grant to Lancaster Symes covered by its description all vacant and unappropriated lands "to the bounds and limits of Richmond County." It did not specify land under air or land under water, but it did set the limits and bounds. It was a correct legal description based upon exact official surveys. To make it definite and certain it specified rivers, runs and streams of water, with fishing rights.

FISH, OYSTERS

AND

CROWN GRANTS.

It is fully and freely admitted by all authorities that the title to all lands under water originally vested and ultimately vest in the Crown.

The presence of water on land has no bearing whatever upon the sovereign's right to grant the land.

History shows that the American Indians made like claims to sovereignty over and title in submerged land. The Indians raised a limited supply of maize or Indian corn, which was to him an important article of food, but his crops, cultivated in a crude fashion, frequently failed or were limited far below his heeds. The Indian looked to the forest for game and pursued the chase; but the winters in colonial times, far more severe than at present, oft times left him shorn of food from the hunt.

The sea, however, never betrayed him; summer and winter and year succeeding year, it furnished him an unfailing supply of fish, while the oyster beds, in close proximity to his settlements on Staten Island, were an unceasing source and furnished an abundant supply of food oysters.

This is clearly and remarkably shown in a very substantial way in the histories of Staten Island, which refer to the period of colonization. They tell

us that adjacent to and over against the sites of the
Indian villages on Staten Island great heaps of oyster
and clam shells were found by the early settlers.
These piles of shells were so extensive that the early
settlers burned them for lime for use in the construction of their houses, and generation after generation
resorted to these deposits of shells as a source of supply for furnishing the much needed lime for Staten
Island lands, used for agricultural purposes.

The lands under water, adjacent to the shores of
Staten Island, were held by the native Indians.

These lands constituted their most important
source of food supply, and would have been fought
for against all trespassers and invaders.

To the Staten Island Indians, the oyster beds of
Staten Island were as important as are the wheat
fields of Minnesota and the Dakotas to the people
of the United States.

The Indians had the same conception of the ownership of uplands, shores and lands under water as
was entertained by European sovereigns. It was the
natural development of that dormant but innate conception of the human mind hereinbefore referred to,
that all titles descend from supreme sovereignty and
that every good thing is a gift from the Great and
Good Spirit.

The South American Indians, under the sway of
the Incas, looked upon their sovereign as representing a dynasty which descended from the sun, or the
supreme God of the heavens. They "out-Heroded
Herod" in exalting the theory of the divine right of
kings into a divinity of kingship. The Indians on the
coast of North America, ruling in their several tribes

the districts about New York, looked to their sovereigns or chiefs and to their councils as representing the title to lands occupied by the tribes.

The Indians of Staten Island, in 1657, in a deed dated July 10th of that year, certified:

> "We, the undersigned natives of North "America, hereditary owners of Staten Island, "certify and declare." (Col. Hist. N. Y., Vol. 14, p. 393.)

In 1658, Wyandance, the famous, peaceable and much beloved Chief of the Montauk Indians, then settled on the east end of Long Island, made a Grant to Lyon Gardiner of the right of herbage on a large tract of land adjoining Southampton. The assent of certain other chiefs or sachems was secured to this Grant.

The chiefs, however, reserved in that Grant "the whales that shall be cast up."

In the year following, the same sachem, Wyandance, granted to the said Gardiner "All whales that might come ashore," on a long extent of sea front.

An interesting fact in connection with this Grant by the Indians to Gardiner is that all whales, with an occasional exception, when stranded or cast up by the sea, are stranded on the outer bar of sand which forms some distance from the shore or on land below low water mark, and on what is known as "land under the deep sea," or submerged lands.

"Royal fish consist of whale and sturgeon, to which the king, or those who have a royal franchise are entitled, when either thrown on the shore or caught near the coast." (Cruise's Digest of the Laws of

England respecting Real Property, 1808, Vol. 2, Title 27.)

In this, as in many other respects, there was perfect harmony between English and American-Indian Common Law.

At a meeting of the Legislative Council of New York held at Fort Henry, March 23rd, 1698, great indignation was there expressed over the fact that Richard Floyd, Jr., had dared to cut up and carry away a dead whale that had drifted ashore on Long Island. The Council declared it "a high contempt of his Majestie's authority and derogatory of his Majestie's right." The Council ordered that the whale be seized and Floyd arrested and prosecuted. It was a bad case of *lese majestie*.

The minutes of the Council for many sessions thereafter show deep resentment over this *poaching upon the Royal fishing preserves*.

A descendant of this man Floyd "got square" with the English Crown, by adding his signature to the historic "Declaration of Independence," in 1776.

In 1726 the Legislative Council of New York approved an act to grant one De Langloisere "the sole fishing of porpoises in the Province of New York during the term of Ten years." Porpoises never invaded the Harbor of New York, though Robbins (Robyns) reef was named after the seal that frequented it in colonial days.

The Fishing Rights granted to Lancaster Symes (1708) were valid under English Common Law and consonant with the custom of the Crown in granting such rights.

In Colonial days whales were exceedingly plentiful

along the New England and Long Island shores, as is clearly shown in the autobiography of Rev. Lyman Beecher, D.D., pastor of the Presbyterian Church of Easthampton, Long Island.

It frequently occurred that whales pursued their food close in to shore, and at high tide would pass in over the outer bar, which bar always forms on that coast beyond where the waves break on the shore. The whales remaining until low tide, would frequently become stranded in the shallow water on the outer bar, when seeking to find their way out into the deep sea. Thereupon the natives on shore would proceed in their canoes to dispatch them and convert them into commercial products.

In fact, whales captured "along shore" by fishermen are generally dispatched and cut up in the water, frequently below low water mark, because of their weight and the depth of water necessary for them in swimming or floating.

With this state of facts clearly before us, we discover that the English recognized in the Indians their rights to the lands under water below low water mark. The settlers seeking to acquire from the Indians this then most fertile source of income and profit on the Atlantic shore, to-wit, the whale fishery, applied to the Indian Chiefs for and received from them Grants to operate an industry which made necessary the occupancy and use of lands under water below low water mark.

There can be no doubt of the fact that the English recognized the Indians' claim of title to such land. The acceptance of such Grants by the settlers, and the English authorities, bound them to such a legal construction.

In one of the foregoing mentioned Grants made by the Indians to the settlers (E. H. R., Vol. 1, p. 148) a limitation is set by the use of a single word in the said Grant, to wit, "Enaughquamuck," which, translated by the Algonkinist authority, William Wallace Tooker, means "as far as the fishing place goes." It is a reasonable deduction that as fishing places are not on dry land, they must extend out and involve the land under water. Here is a definite recognition of title to land under water claimed as belonging to and granted by the Indians. Further evidence, in support of the Indians' claim to the lands under water at their fishing places and elsewhere is the ever recurring expression in histories of colonial times, "the fishing grounds of the Indians." It is a pertinent inquiry, Why did the natives, the colonists, and the colonial and imperial authorities constantly refer to the "Indians' fishing grounds" if they only meant the waters in which they fished? As conclusive proof of the Indians' claim, and maintenance of title, to lands under water below low water mark, we cite the case of Fisher's Island, situated at the Eastern end of Long Island Sound, the title to which Island, and the fishing grounds surrounding the Island, were claimed and held by the Rhode Island Indians as against all comers.

There is a small stream on the eastern end of Long Island by the name of Wading River. Its Indian name was "Pauquacumsuck," which signifies "the brook or outlet where we wade for clams." This is a tidal stream. It flows into the sea or sound. It was planted by the Indians with clams. It was a source, and an important one, of the Indians' food supply and its name appears in grants and deeds.

"What is planted in the soil belongs to the soil."

The identification of the fishing grounds as an integral part of Indian lands and lands of the early settlers is interestingly referred to in the recent decision of the New York Court of Appeals, in the case of Lillius Grace vs. Town of North Winsted (Feb. 26th, 1916), in which the Court recites the attraction possessed by Long Island for settlers, caused by the shell fish abounding in its tidal waters and which belonged to and were a part of its submerged lands.

It also referred to the Grants and to "the extrinsic facts as to the situation of the colony." It reached the conclusion that the patents embraced the lands under the bay.

The subject of Crown Grants of lands under water is thoroughly and comprehensively discussed in the leading case of Rodgers vs. Jones (1 John 237). This case has been uniformly followed and is recognized as controlling in New York State. Rodgers was sued by one Jones, a surveyor of the Town of Oyster Bay, for the recovery of a penalty created by the by-laws of the Town, which declared "that no person not being an inhabitant of Oyster Bay shall be allowed to rake or take any oysters on the creeks or harbors of the Town of Oyster Bay, under the penalty of $12.50 for each offense."

The Town claimed title under an English Crown Grant. The penalty was enforced by the trial court and the judgment was affirmed on an appeal. The description contained in the Grant under which the

Town of Oyster Bay asserted its right is in nowise as comprehensive as the description contained in the final and inclusive Grant made by the English Crown closing out the Crown's estate on Staten Island to Lancaster Symes.

"It has, however, been strenuously but mistakenly insisted that the right of alienation by the Crown was restricted by *Magna Charta* and other statutes, not only so as to prevent the King from making a Grant of a fishery in severalty but from making any absolute transfer of the soil under water."

"What may be the law elsewhere on the strength of reasoning sustaining this view, it must be regarded as the law of New York that no such restraints were imposed by the *Magna Charta* or otherwise upon the kingly power." (Estates and Rights of the Corp. of the City of N. Y., Vol. 1, p. 223.)

Fisheries are of three kinds:

> *First,*   Several.
> *Second,* Free.
> *Third,*   Common.

"The right of 'several' fisheries, as already shown, is founded on and annexed to the soil and is, by reason of, and concommittance with the ownership of the soil. When the soil of a navigable river is granted, the right of 'several' fisheries therein begins." (Words and Phrases Judicially Defined, "Fishery.")

"The right to fish and take fish is not an easement; it is a right of profit in lands." (Wickham vs. Hawker, 7M 7W 73.)

"A fishery is in the river and is not the space between high and low water mark, though the use of that space may be necessary in the use of it and may be included in the term." (Tinicum Fishing Co. vs. Carter, 61 Pa. 21, 37.)

"A fishing pool or place is defined by statute to be from the place or places where the seins or nets have been usually thrown into the water to the place or places where they have been usually taken out." (Tinicum Fishing Co. vs. Carter, 61 Pa. 21, 36.)

"The term 'Royal Fishery' at common law was used to designate the right of fishery in a navigable river in which the sea ebbed and flowed, and was so called *because the right was a part of the prerogative of the King.*" (Arnold vs. Mundy, 6 N. J. Law (1 Halst) 1, 86.)

"A free fishery or exclusive right of fishing in a public river is a royal franchise, which is now frequently vested in private persons, either by Grant *from the Crown* or by prescription." (Cruise's Digest of the Laws of England Respecting Real Property (1808), Vol. 2, Tit. 27.)

The theory of English Common Law, elucidated by Blackstone and other authorities, that in the granting of the land and the conveyance of same, the presence or nonpresence of water thereon is not taken into account is in strict harmony with the decisions of the English Courts, contemporaneous with and subsequent to the Crown Grants of land on Staten Island relating to fisheries, as made in 1708 to Lancaster Symes.

On November 13th, 1799, the English Crown brought an action for the restoration of a certain M. Harman to an office in a company from which it appears he had been devolved. This is a case known as "the King vs. the Stewart, foreman, treasurer, bookkeeper, and freeman of the Company, of free fishermen, and dredgemen, of the manor and hundred of Faversham, in the County of Kent." In the course of the proofs, and as collateral evidence in sustaining the principal contentions in the case, it was shown that the Lord of the said Manor who had received his Manor by Grant of land from the Crown, held title to the Oyster beds, or Oyster Grounds under the tidal waters adjacent thereto.

It was further disclosed in that case that the company of free fishermen and dredgemen of the Manor, held of the Lord of the Manor, the said Oyster Grounds. It was also shown in that case, that in order to preclude any doubt as to the Oyster Grounds being subject to the Crown Grant of land and controlled thereby, and that the dredging of oysters thereon was not a common right of the people; "Every person admitted to the freedom (of the Manor) hath before his admission taken an oath that he would be a true tenant to the Lord for the fishing grounds."

It appears that this right of oyster dredging which was claimed and held by the Lord of the manor was held by him under his land Grant, and that the company of free fishermen and dredgemen "held of the lord of said Manor and hundred, certain oyster grounds within the said Manor and hundred, and during all that time have laid and kept oysters upon the said ground for the common use and benefit of the said company." The right of the Crown to have made the Grant and the right of the Lord of the

Manor to have made a Grant to the company of fishermen and dredgemen under his land Grant was admitted and not traversed by either party to the action.
The three learned judges thereupon gave opinions as
follows:

> "Upon this state of the case the Court will
> "consider that the fishery and the soil pass to-
> "gether." (*Chief Justice Lord Mansfield.*)

> "There is no doubt but that a fishery is a tene-
> "ment. Trespass will lie for an injury to it and
> "it may be recovered in ejectment." (*Judge
> Ashhurst.*)

> "The fact of letting a fishery is sufficient and
> "we must presume that the soil pass along with
> "it." (*Judge Buller.*)

> (King vs. Alresford (1786), Court of
> King's Bench, Durnford and East's Report,
> Vol. 1, 360-1.)

The above named three Judges constituted one, if
not the ablest judicial triumvirate that ever held
court in England sitting together on the same bench.

> The bounds of the Manor of Faversham in
> Kent, England, are thus given (Hasted, Vol.
> VI, page 335):

> "The Town and parish of Faversham, the
> "boroughs of Harty, Ore, Ewell, Selgrave, Old-
> "gold, Scheld, Chetham, Brinnystone, Badles-
> "mere, Oldebonde Island, Roda Graveyney,

"Bourdefield and the lands of Moukendans, in "the parish of Moukton."

It will be noticed that Oldebonde Island is described simply as an Island. *It should also be observed that the Court of the Kings Bench held in the case referred to above, that the oyster beds in the waters about the Island were included in and covered by the Grant of the land as on the Island even though the Grant contained no reference to submerged lands or lands under water.*

"The customs of Kent are a part of the old "Common Law." (Tenures of Kent, page 77.)

The Court of Kings Bench was a royal Court, the Justices of which decided the King's causes, i. e., those affecting the King's Crown and dignity. This Court had no fixed place for holding its sessions, but held Court where the King happened to be. Originally the King himself sat with the Court and passed upon the issues involved. (Crab's History of English Law.)

In the case of the Trustees of Brookhaven vs. Strong (60 N. Y. 56-73), the New York Court of Appeals set forth at considerable length the right of fishery under an English Crown Grant. The issue raised was as to the right of the Town of Brookhaven in and to certain oyster beds in the Great South Bay, where such right was not precisely defined in the language of the Grant. The Court, near the conclusion of its very comprehensive opinion, says:

"Besides the language of the patents, 'all riv-
"ers, waters, beaches, creeks, harbors, fishing
"and all other franchises to said tracts apper-
"taining' *is significant of an intention to convey*
"*this very right. There is no reason why these*
"*terms should not be construed according to*
"*their ordinary meaning, especially when ap-*
"*plied to land under water included within the*
"*boundaries.*"

Nothing is more certain than a certainty. Therefore, how redundant is the description contained in
the Crown Grant to Lancaster Symes and how comprehensively it applies to the Staten Island Oyster
Beds, in the light of the foregoing decisions. We
read from the Symes Grant, among many other
rights conveyed, the following:

"All meadows, marshes, swamps, pooles,
"ponds, waters, brooks, fishing and fowling,
"hunting and hawking," the same "lyeing or be-
"ing or to be had, used or enjoyed in them, the
"bounds and limitts aforesaid, and all other
"profitts, benefitts, advantages, hereditaments
"and appurtenances whatsoever unto the said
"pieces and parcells of land and premises be-
"longing or in anywise appurteying."

"The bounds and limitts," referred to were
the therein before expressed "bounds and lim-
"itss of Richmond County."

In the case of Robins vs. Ackerly (91 N. Y. 98)
the language of the Grant as made to the Town of

Huntington is much narrower in its application to fishing rights than is the language of the Symes Staten Island Grant. In that case, however, the Court construed the Grant as applying to Northport Harbor, with its oyster beds.

In the case of the Town of Southampton vs. Mecox Bay Oyster Co. (116 N. Y. 1), the Court construed the Crown Grant to the Town of Southampton as including the oyster beds under the waters of the Bay. In that Grant also, the language applied to fishing is far more limited in its scope than is the language contained in the Crown Grant to Lancaster Symes, under which all remaining Crown lands on Staten Island were conveyed to him.

> "A right to take fish, including *shell fish* in "the sea and in the arms and bays thereof and "in rivers where the tide ebbs and flows, below "high water mark is common to all citizens, *un-* "*less restrained by some act* on the part of the "Government or State having sovereignty over "the same."

> "*An individual may acquire* the right to fish "in a creek or river to the exclusion of the pub- "lic *by the King's Grant.*" (Washburne, on Easements and Servitudes, pp. 410, 412.)

> "*The bed of all navigable rivers* where the "tide flows and reflows and of all estuaries or "arms of the sea *is by law vested in the Crown.*" (Gann vs. The Free Fishers of Whitstable, House of Lords 11, H. L. C. 192, Lord Westbury.)

"*The right of the Sovereign* exists in every
"navigable river where the sea ebbs and flows.
"*Every such river is a royal river and the fishing*
"*of it is a royal fishery* and belongs to the Queen
"by her prerogatives." (Neill vs. Duke of Devonshire, 8 App. Cas. (135) 157 Lord
O'Hagan.)

"The private right of fishery ceases to exist
"below the point where the right of the Crown
"to the soil commences." (Doss on Law of Riparian Rights, 90.)

THE GRIP

OF

CROWN GRANTS

It has been clearly established that the English Crown had a good and perfect title to all lands on and about Staten Island, in the State of New York.

The Crown's title included all lands above water and all lands under water together with all lands between high and low water mark in the County of Richmond.

This proposition is absolutely correct.

It was a complete and perfect title as a proposition of law. It covered every square foot of land from the highest point on the uplands to the most submerged soil in the rivers, bays and seas, to the utmost limits and bounds of Richmond County.

Not one square foot of land within the present County of Richmond was exempt or escaped from the grasp and grip of that Royal Title. Not one foot of land within the County's boundaries but originally belonged to the Royal estate. Each and every title descends from and rests upon the Crown's purchase of Staten Island from the Indian inhabitants thereof as well as upon the right of discovery.

The Crown held, through the Duke of York's purchase, all lands owned by the Indians of Staten Island and closed out to its grantees all that it had so acquired. The language of the Symes Grant is conclusive and *thereafter the Crown never again exercised a single right or claim of ownership to lands in Richmond County* in the State of New York.

The Crown Lands on Staten Island constituted one solid and unbroken estate under one Imperial proprietorship. It was the personal estate of the English Crown. The Crown owned every right, title and use in and pertaining to the fee and was in complete possession thereof.

The English Crown could have permitted its subjects to cultivate the lands; erect houses thereon, establish ferries therefrom or thereto. It could have also granted the right to fish, hawk and hunt thereon, cultivate and dig oysters in the seas and bays thereof; or it could have refused or denied each and every such privilege. No English citizens would have questioned such indulgence or forbearance by their Sovereign.

The English Crown was the owner of the lands in fee, pure and simple as an individual proprietor. What is more, and it is a very important historical fact, it undertook to and did attach Staten Island to the Crown's personal Manor of East Greenwich in the County of Kent, England. Staten Island by such Royal act became an integral part of that Manor to which for a long time legal accountings were made of all revenues received therefrom by the Crown's agents pursuant to the terms of the Crown Grants issued for lands thereon.

Individual and personal rights and privileges belonging to the Crown as the personal owner of the Manor of East Greenwich in the County of Kent,

England, also belonged to the Crown as the personal owner of Staten Island. If the Crown could sell the one it could sell the other. It could lease its country estate at East Greenwich, and it could lease its lands on Staten Island. While the Sovereign was King or Queen that same Sovereign was also Lord or Lady of the Manor of East Greenwich in the County of Kent. Staten Island, while under the political jurisdiction of the Crown was the personal property of the Lord or Lady of the Manor of East Greenwich.

The laws governing and protecting proprietorship of manorial lands in England, whether owned by prince or plebian, likewise threw their protection over title to lands in the province of New York, whether held by the Sovereign or the settler, as a part of a personal and individual estate.

The above being true, we turn to an investigation of the various English Crown Grants made by the English crown to lands on Staten Island based upon the indisputable title vested in the English Crown, as Lord or Lady of the Manor.

To understand the rights and privileges covered and included in the Crown Grants to lands on Staten Island three acts are desirable. yea, in fact are essential:

> *First*—Seal up or dismiss from all consideration every statute enacted since the year 1708, whether by Parliament, Province, State or Federal Government.
>
> *Second*—Use profound discrimination in reading the decisions of the English, State and Federal Courts.

Third—In so far as they *interpret* the common law
of England from 1635 to 1708 they apply
and govern. Vested rights acquired in that
period cannot be adversely affected by any
subsequent changes in statutory or common
law rights in property.

Remember that the facts must be similar if the
decision is to control.

All of the Grants made by the Crown of England
to lands on Staten Island were apparently *leases in
form,* but were *deeds in fact.* They were all subject
to the payment of annual "quit-rents," representing
a strict condition that the grantee should pay to the
Crown a certain fixed sum each year or forfeit possession thereof at the will of the Crown. The failure to pay the quit-rents entitled the Crown to re-
enter and take possession of the land theretofore
granted.

A Crown Grant did not become void upon failure
to pay the quit-rents until notice of forfeiture was
served by the Crown upon the Grantee and proper
legal proceedings were completed, to vacate the Grant
or nullify the same.

It has been judicially decided that this rental condition "ran with the land." The Grant when properly recorded, gave good and sufficient public notice
that the Grantee's right of occupancy or possession under his title absolutely depended upon the
payment by him of the stipulated quit-rents. Notice
of a default in quit-rents and a notice of the cancellation of the Grant by the Crown was necessary to
make the Grant void. Proceedings in court must

then be undertaken by the Crown in order to re-obtain possession.

The term "quit-rents" was simply another name for rents. When the Grantee paid the quit rent it "quit the rent" for the period covered by the payment.

"Pay rent, keep possession;
"Default in rent, lose possession."

This is a maxim relating to leases which is too well understood by all generations to need any amplification here. The same rule applied to Grants of lands or deeds thereto which were subject to even nominal rental.

Certain conditions were necessary to make a Grant complete, valid and not subject to forfeiture.

(a)   It must be dated.
(b)   It must be patented.
(c)   Its quit rents must be regularly paid, or its quit rents must be commuted; that is paid in advance by one inclusive payment.

There were over one hundred and fifty English Crown Grants issued by the Crown, to lands on Staten Island. These Grants may be classified in eight distinct groups or classes:

(Class A)   Grants under which rents were paid until further payments were commuted under New York Statutes, by a cash payment in full. Titles in fee and clear.

(Class B)   Grants under which quit rents were paid for a time, but payments then ceased. They were not commuted. Rights of forfeiture of titles and repossession of lands thereby accrued under the terms of the original Grants.

(Class C)   Grants under which no quit rents were paid. Right of forfeiture of titles and repossession of lands thereby accrued under the terms of the original Grants.

(Class D)   Grants which were made but not confirmed by Council. No titles passed. No quit rents were paid. Confirmation of Grants was necessary to their legality and payment of quit rents was required under the terms of the original Grants.

(Class E)   Grants which were prepared but not dated and not patented. No quit rents were paid. No titles passed.

(Class F)   Grants which were prepared but not dated and not patented. No titles passed. Pending the uncertainty as to the issue of the patents, some small quit rents were paid.

(Class G)   Grants which were not recorded until after the Grant to Lancaster Symes had been made, issued and recorded covering all vacant and unappropriated lands within the limits and bounds of Richmond County.

Class G Grants were as follows:

1st   To Adriensen from *a former Grantee* of the Crown.

2nd   To Dusachoy, consented to
by Lancaster Symes and confirmed by the Crown.

3rd   To Jorissee from former
grantee of the Crown.
It was a common custom for
a Grantee when holding land
under a Crown Grant to file
a request with the Crown to
issue a Grant to his customer
or sub-grantee. This gave
such a sub-grantee a Royal
Grant direct from the Sovereign and released the original Grantee.

4th   To Bellue and Dove. A 20
year lease by Lancaster
Symes of Shore front on
Sand Bay for Ferry pur-
poses, and a ferry franchise
from the Crown.

5th   To Shotwell. This was a
Royal confirmation of a title
by adverse possession "upward of 35 years."
As forty years adverse possession was necessary to obtain a title against the
Crown, this Grant was made

by directions from Symes or
by his consent.

(Class H)   This class covers only the Crown
Grant to Lancaster Symes.   Quit
rents were paid until commuted under the New York Statutes by a cash
payment in full, which commutation
was in effect under the law a new
Grant to Lancaster Symes from the
State of New York.   The commutation of quit rents has been judicially
decided as being in legal effect, the
issue of a New Grant.   (Class H is
the same in every respect as Class
A.)

By a comparison of this schedule with the map of
classified lands on Staten Island, due reference being
had to the conditions set forth herein as necessary to
make a Crown Grant legal and valid, the reader can
readily understand where the legal title to any and
every piece of land on Staten Island rested after the
final and inclusive Grant was made by the English
Crown to Lancaster Symes in 1708.   This Grant to
Lancaster Symes covered and included all lands not
previously granted and patented.

Whatever titles to lands in Richmond County were
then (1708) vested in the English Crown and which
it had the right to grant away, it did grant to Lancaster Symes.

It has been found that many Grants were applied
for but were not issued by the Crown; many other
Grants having been applied for were issued by the

Crown, but were not patented by the Grantees. Many other Grants went through such formalities but the Grantee paid no quit rents thereunder. Other errors and omissions are clearly shown of record, which rendered nugatory and of no legal force or effect certain other Grants.

It is now possible for the State of New York to cure these defects by exercising its right of forfeiture of and re-entry upon the lands affected by such errors and defaults. Thereupon *it might regrant such lands to the present record owners thereof* and every cloud would vanish from land titles on Staten Island where such defects are created by the difficulties enumerated here.

Class A Grants—These Crown Grants were perfect. They were duly issued, properly dated and patented. The quit rents thereunder were paid up to the time when they were subsequently commuted. That is, all quit rents thereunder were paid for a time and then the State of New York, after the Revolutionary War, accepted one payment in full of all further demands whereupon all rents ceased. It has been judicially determined that the complete settlement of quit rents under a Crown Grant by a payment in advance, of an agreed sum, in full payment therefor converts such a title into a complete fee. It has been likewise determined that the acceptance of such a payment by the State is equivalent to and "constitutes a new Grant in fee, by the State." *The acceptance of such a payment by the State deprives the State of any right thereafter to challenge the validity and regularity of such Grant.*

There appears to be but two Crown Grants on

Staten Island which can be properly included in Class A. *One of the two Grants referred to is the Crown Grant to Lancaster Symes, but which Grant, because of its extent, has been specially listed in Class H.*

Class B Grants—The Grantees in this classification received their Grants and patented the same. They paid their quit rents for a time, but subsequently defaulted thereon and ceased to pay. As these Grants were issued conditional upon the payment by the Grantee of annual rentals and as the quit rents were not paid as required under the terms of the Grant, the Crown's right of forfeiture and re-entry accrued, which right is now vested in the State of New York.

Class C Grants—The Grantees in this class went through the proper forms of having their Grants issued, dated and patented, but no quit rents were ever paid thereunder. The consideration for the issue of these Class C Grants was the payment of quit rents and rentals thereunder were never paid. All of the Grants in this class became and in fact always were null and void and of no effect. "No title or interest in lands can pass under any instrument where a good and valid consideration is not paid."

Class D Grants—The titles in this class are even more striking in their defects. The parties securing these Grants apparently not caring to pay the quit rents or perchance having changed their minds as to the desired locations did not patent their Grants. As a fundamental proposition of law, a Grant must be patented to be valid. The Grants in this class not having been patented no quit rents were paid thereunder. Such being the case the Grants themselves were never completed. This vital and fundamental defect renders these so-called Grants as if never applied for.

Class E Grants—The Grants in this class were prepared by the Crown, but evidently awaiting some proper action by the Grantees, were not even dated. Not being dated, and no rents or consideration having been paid thereunder, they were clearly and plainly null and void, and of no effect from their very inception.

No date, no consideration, no patent means beyond cavil *no Grant.*

Class F Grants—The Grants in this class, for some undisclosed reasons, were held up by the Crown. They were not dated nor patented. The Grantees made a few payments to the English Crown in anticipation of receiving a Grant, or as was frequently done in those days, they rented for one or a few seasons certain pasturage or tillable lands and then quit the use or occupancy thereof without the issue to them of a Grant.

Not having been issued or patented and the rentals having ceased, no rights as Grantees ever accrued thereunder.

Class G Grants—As above explained, these Grants were recorded after the Crown Grant to Lancaster Symes was recorded. They were Grants made subject to the rights and consent of Lancaster Symes, as previously explained in this chapter or of lands which had been granted by the Crown previous to its Grant to Lancaster Symes.

Class H Grants—This is the Grant to Lancaster

Symes and is on a parity with and is properly included in *Class A Grants*.

In the light of the foregoing statement covering every English Crown Grant issued to lands on Staten Island we turn to a map of the Island on which there has been clearly outlined the above classified lands. This map of classified lands is based upon a map of Crown Grants prepared by official surveyors on which map every English Crown Grant to lands on Staten Island is located, by metes and bounds.

We have followed with great care the official records and the map prepared by the Government Surveyors in order that the information disclosed on this classified map might rest upon official documentary proof and be in no wise a conjecture, or the expression of an individual judgment or opinion on the part of the author.

We simply submit the historic proofs at hand for what they may be worth for use in clearing up the titles to lands on Staten Island.

On the map of lands which we have classified according to information obtained by us from official sources we show the relation of all titles to lands on Staten Island at the close of the year 1708 as such titles appear related to the Original English Crown Grants from which they did or supposedly did descend.

It is a pertinent inquiry as to whether any of the Grantees referred to, who were in default in payment of their quit rents, continued to occupy and possess the lands which may have been taken over by them under their respective Grants.

Adverse possession as against the Crown required

forty years of continuous occupancy under strict and arbitrary conditions difficult to perform and the performance of which is more difficult to prove.

With this possibility in view, we examined with great care other proper public records and discovered that practically all of the Grantees, so in default, never gave a deed or lease to any other person or persons of the lands described in their respective Grants. Neither do we find the lands so referred to included as an asset in their respective estates at their decease.

It is a very proper conclusion that the Grantees (a) whose lands were not patented, and (b) who failed to pay any of their quit rents, and (c) who issued no leases or deeds therefor during their lifetime, and (d) whose estates failed to include as an asset lands referred to, *either never took physical possession of the lands included in such Grants, or then abandoned the land.* In fact, failure to occupy, or abandonment, speak out from a vast majority of the Staten Island Crown Grants issued by the English Crown, under Class B Grants to Class G Grants inclusive.

This reasonable presumption is not only sustained by the public records, but is supported by historical authorities. Many of the early English settlers abandoned their lands and moved to New Jersey and Pennsylvania, where they took up other lands. Many others, descendants of original Grantees, being loyalists, took the side of England in the Revolutionary War and fled when peace was made. Much land was thereby abandoned, while other land was escheated by the State of New York for treason.

In 1708 the Crown closed out to Lancaster Symes all of the Crown lands within "the bounds and limits of Richmond County," New York.

It is in no wise strange that after the treatment the English Crown had received from a large majority of its Staten Island Grantees, it should have closed out its title therein to "its loyal and faithful subject," Lancaster Symes. It is not intended by the foregoing statement to even imply that at the present time all of the lands so originally included under Class B Grants to Class G Grants, inclusive, descended to and are now possessed by the present owner of the Lancaster Symes title. Such a theory would be contrary to the fact, unfair, unjust, and hurtful to many innocent and true owners of much of the lands so referred to.

There are two distinct ways by which lands originally granted, and which we have included in Class H Grants, may have become the properties of parties in no wise interested in the original Crown Grants and who can now claim no direct descent of title therefrom.

The record title should, however, be traceable back to an original Crown Grant to avert danger of defeat under even an apparently strong claim of adverse possession on the part of those now in possession or from whom their claim of title may descend. Even to establish a title by adverse possession such a transcript of record is very desirable.

Titles may have been obtained through the medium of tax sales. If any of the lands covered by and included in the original Crown Grants *have been duly and properly assessed* and the owners thereof

have defaulted in the payment of taxes thereon, and
if such properties *have thereafter been properly exposed for sale* and *properly and legally sold for taxes
in strict conformity with the statutes,* then the title
thereto may have passed by virtue of such tax sale to
parties other than the original owners or their descendants in title of record.

> In matters of tax sales, "the State proceeds in
> "a summary way to seize and appropriate the
> "property of the citizen *in invitum,* and the sale
> "and conveyance are but steps in the proceeding
> "which must be shown to have been duly insti-
> "tuted and regularly prosecuted, or the at-
> "tempted confiscation will fail unless there is
> "some statute which makes the deed presumptive
> "or conclusive evidence of regularity." (Da-
> lancey vs. Piepgras 138, N. Y. 26.)

In view, however, of the manner in which assess-
ments and tax sales were conducted up to within a
very short period on Staten Island the average tax
title, acquired by virtue of a tax sale, is somewhat of
the nature of "a snair and delusion," and is easily set
aside by a proper procedure, if we correctly judge
the record.

Parties now in possession of lands included in and
covered by any of the Original Crown Grants and
who cannot in any wise trace their chain of titles back
to the Crown Grants originally covering the lands
they occupy, may be able to show a good and valid
title to the lands referred to through adverse possession on their part or from some one from whom their
title descended who was able to and did clearly show

such proof of adverse possession as permitted under the law.

The statutes of the State clearly provide a method by which title to a property actually owned by another may be obtained by adverse possession under certain circumstances and conditions.

The procedure under such legislation and the method to be pursued in order to obtain such a title are very clearly and distinctly prescribed in the Statutes, while the decisions of the courts are very consistent as to what is necessary to establish a title by adverse possession.

It is obnoxious to the law and contrary to conscience or equity that a man shall knowingly and in a hostile manner seize upon, take possession of, and hold property that is not his own, and by such procedure divest the lawful owner thereof of his rights therein, to the benefit and enrichment of the party who by legal force and violence obtained possession thereof.

> Judges shrink from decreeing that a moral wrong, from age and persistence therein, has become a legal right.

The state of mind, however, which protests against a practice which in itself is of the nature of larceny is mollified and altered to a degree by mitigating and extenuating circumstances. In order that a member of society shall transform an act that was originally of the nature of a legal and moral wrong into an act that is to be tolerated, permitted and approved by a Court of Justice or Equity, the party thereto is sternly required to strictly comply with severe conditions laid down by the law.   To maintain a title based upon adverse possession is a difficult task and presents an issue which, though tolerated, is not welcomed in the Halls of Justice and Equity.

It is therefore not strange that Title Companies in the majority of instances refuse to guarantee titles obtained by adverse possession or tax sales, and conservative money lenders turn from such titles as too hazardous a security for loans.

The American Title and Trust Company, the recent record owner of the titles to land on Staten Island descending from and through Lancaster Symes, had no purpose nor did it desire to deprive any one of the possession of lands on Staten Island if such an one had properly and lawfully obtained his title by adverse possession, legal tax sale, or in any other manner approved by the law of the land or the conscience of the community.

The Title Company referred to, upon satisfying itself of such a state of facts in any particular instance, proposed to frankly and unhesitatingly admit and recognize the same, regardless of original wrongful trespass upon and violent assertion of a forcible possession of lands of which it had been so deprived.

To illustrate this latter conclusion, we cite the following instance:

The American Title and Trust Company was called upon by a citizen of Staten Island whose chief and practically only estate is a comfortable house in which he lives and a few acres of land on Staten Island favorably situated and upon which his house is located.

The elderly man informed the Title Company that

he had suffered from many sleepless nights since the acquisition by the American Title and Trust Company of the Symes title to lands on Staten Island. He said that he knew that the land he occupied had belonged to Lancaster Symes. He further stated that he "wanted to be true and honest with all men and that he did not wish to die holding lands which were in fact not his own." He further remarked that he "wanted no trouble to occur after his decease over his small possession." With this statement he offered to surrender the title to his home and so "square his conscience" with the world.

The American Title and Trust Company knew as a proposition of law that this honest old citizen had in fact acquired a good and perfect legal possessory right to his home, by adverse possession. It so informed him and explained to him the law. He was shown that in the first instance Lancaster Symes had a perfect title to the plot of ground referred to, but that now under the Statutes of the State of New York, such right of possession had ceased. Therefore, the American Title and Trust Company refused to accept the tender of the deed on the theory that it would be depriving the old gentleman of property that was lawfully possessed by him and to which the Title Company had no legal or equitable claim. "He who asks equity must do equity." The officers of the Title Company, somewhat like the old man, wanted their consciences "square with the world."

Adverse possession cannot be obtained by the State or by the City, but only by such private citizens and corporations who for not less than twenty years in some instances and for not less than forty years in

other circumstances have strictly complied with the
very stringent law, under which definite and complete proof necessary to maintain adverse possession
is difficult and trying to establish.   While such adverse possession may be a fact, the proof thereof as
prescribed by law and insisted upon by the courts is
exceedingly difficult in the majority of instances.

TITLE GUARANTEES

AND

CROWN GRANTS.

The Book entitled "THE MAJOR AND THE QUEEN" was written that it might rescue from almost complete oblivion the name and reputation of Major Lancaster Symes, a prominent character in the Colonial History of the Province of New York.

Major Lancaster Symes died possessed of an extensive estate. He was the owner of more than one half of Staten Island. His property interests at the time of his decease were very widespread. They included possessions in Holland, hereditary rights in England and real estate in several counties in the Province of New York.

No Crown Grant to Lancaster Symes covering lands in any other County in the State of New York has ever been voided, nor has his Richmond County Grant ever been traversed.

During the past several years the author of this narrative has been making a successful international search for records and documents relating to Major Lancaster Symes.

These efforts resulted in remarkable disclosures. The awe-inspiring mystery with which vivid imaginations had cloaked the name and fame of Major Symes has been completely dispelled. In the brighter light of recently revealed history there stands before the mind the historic picture of a gallant officer and a loyal and true citizen who was the owner of a valuable estate, a portion of which was located on Staten Island. He died, having bequeathed his property to his family.

He died fully trusting that the conscience and the laws of the public which he had so faithfully defended and served, would safeguard his posterity in their rightful inheritance.

The generation in which he had lived remembered him with affection and the following generation honored his memory. Then the stern resolve and defiance of the Colonists hurled at the English Crown precipitated the American Revolutionary War, in the wild excitement of which much that was English was execrated.

The Colonists had little time or thought for the memory of the dead English soldier or for that of earlier generations, when fighting two of their battles in the very churchyard and Colonial burying ground given by this same Lancaster Symes to St. Andrew's Church and in which "God's Acre" slept many of their own sacred dead.

The passions of war smothered the impulses of gratitude.

St. Andrew's Protestant Episcopal Church in Richmond, Staten Island, which Major Symes had generously aided by gifts of lands, became a war hospital, a battle ground and fuel for battle flames. Some of its English members were driven into exile for not espousing the cause of the Colonists. Others of its friends were banished under sentence of death

for loyalty to their Mother Country.   The rejuv-
enated St. Andrew's Church, having been previously
rent, torn and impoverished for a time by war de-
spoilment and flames, forgot its benefactor.   It even
dreamed that he belonged to the myths.   His memory
so completely faded from its recollections that for
generations it appears to have lost all thought of him
in connection with a large acreage of land received
by it as a gift from Major Lancaster Symes, notwithstanding the fact that the deed conveying such endowment was clearly recorded within two hundred
feet of the parish house.

If the Church, the receiver of his substantial bene-
factions, could so forget its benefactor, is it at all
strange that after the passions of Revolutionary War
and the troubles of reconstructing social order at its
close, the public should also have forgotten him, a
faithful public servant?

Many tracts of Staten Island lands were sold and
transferred, immediately subsequent to the Grant
made to Lancaster Symes in 1708.   Such operations
in real estate have continued on Staten Island down
to the present time, a period of over two centuries.

According to official records in the County Seat of
Richmond County, not a map showing one single
transfer of lands on Staten Island appears of record
in the County Clerk's Office for one century following the Grant to Symes.   Not a map of record in that
County Seat showing the transfer of any Staten
Island real estate for a period of over one hundred
years!

For a time following that absolute void of one century in the map records in Richmond County, such

maps as were filed covered but small plots of land and single farms.   In many cases such maps did not even adequately or clearly represent the descriptions in the deeds to which they referred.

One of the most respected, conservative and progressive of Title Companies recently made public an announcement that it will not make guaranteed searches of titles to lands on Staten Island *extending back to the original Crown Grants*.

This is seemingly a strange policy to be announced or pursued by such a representative Title Company, but as the author understands the situation, it is in harmony with a policy quite uniformly adopted by other Title Companies doing business on Staten Island.

The situation as to many of the titles to Staten Island real estate, however, demanded such an attitude. Title Company officers, directors and counsel acting as trustees for interests they represent must take notice of and be governed by conditions as they exist.   The amazing attitude of public officialdom down to within a recent "handbreadth" of time has been based upon the incorrect theory that no official survey of Staten Island has been made in the past and that the Island has not been mapped.

The records of Richmond County fail to show any complete official survey of Staten Island.   We have stated that for a space of one century (1710-1810) not a map is there recorded covering any transfer of lands on Staten Island, though history and official books of record show a steady conveyance of real property.

The deeds and mortgages recorded during that

period fill book after book, but no maps are recorded accompanying the same.

It is thought by many that there were some maps prepared and filed during that time in Richmond, the County Seat, but that in several fires which occurred there and which destroyed many valuable records, the maps representing that period of time were consumed.

Be that as it may, the fact remains that no maps representing land transfers for over one century are now of record in the County Seat.

An examination of Staten Island deeds recorded at the County Seat disclosed a very curious state of facts. The description in a deed may run from a "small pile of stones," now scattered, to an "elm tree," now destroyed. It then may take a turn to a "brook," the name of which is lost or was never generally known or preserved of record. Then the described boundary wanders, perchance, to a "salt meadow," said on the record to belong to a person named therein but who, upon examination of Liber or Book of Deeds does not appear as an owner of record of any real estate on the Island.

The description in a deed taken at random from the Richmond County Public Records runs as follows:

A certain party, "an Attorney at Law," purports to sell to another party, a "Doctor of Physic," a certain piece of land "once owned by" a certain named and doubtlessly then highly respected female. No description by "metes and bounds" accompanies this last mentioned deed. No public record shows that the said "Attorney at Law" ever owned it or had any right to sell it. The nearest approach to a declared ownership in the property is the disingenuous statement that a certain female "once owned" it, but no public record shows such ownership on her part.

The lawyer purported to sell it to a "Doctor of Physic" as eighty acres. The "Doctor of Physic" gave a deed the following day for one hundred acres. The plot kept expanding on the records by systematic "accretions" due to vivid imaginations or cumulative cupidity combined with "remarkable descriptive powers," until it became a comely estate. First it extended to a salt meadow; at the next turn it extended to the beach. Following that it absorbed the land between high and low water mark. The last heard of it was that it had extended out to sea, and submarine fashion was moving out along the bottom of the Great Deep. It is too deep for us to fathom.

Present titles (?) to that property rest upon an erstwhile "lawyer" and a "doctor of physic," buying and selling lands said to have belonged to another, while the records fail to show either one of them ever owned any portion of the land in question.

Is it strange that one of three title searchers recently conferring together in the County Seat, after looking up the record of still another piece of land on Staten Island, remarked in desperation, "Well, between the three of us we ought to be able to 'dope' out some kind of a title to this piece of land."

Why does such a situation exist? It is intolerable! The excellent Title Companies represented in Richmond County have been a powerful influence in helping to steady public confidence and have greatly aided real estate business in a multitude of cases. They have made possible sales and loans that otherwise would not have been realized. Every real estate operator and every Title Company conversant with all the facts, together with the legally constituted public officials in Richmond, fully realize the deplorable conditions existing as to the records of early titles on Staten Island.

The English Crown owned Staten Island—*every foot of it*. It issued a series of Crown Grants thereof to private individuals and closed out all of the Crown's ownership in Staten Island—*every foot of it.*

Instead of "no survey having been made of Staten Island," a complete survey of the Island was made by the English Crown and the official map thereof is in the possession of and is owned by the American Title and Trust Company. The same Company has also an official location of each and every English Crown Grant shown on a map of Staten Island, prepared by official surveyors. It has also an official record of each and every Grant, showing the dates of their issue and other essential facts affecting the descent or non-descent of titles therefrom. It has also certified copies of the Grants covering lands granted on Staten Island by the English Crown.

These facts relate to every square foot of land on Staten Island to the utmost "bounds and limits of Richmond County." The information covers the seas, bays and rivers included by the United States Government, the State of New Jersey and the State of New York within the defined and fixed boundaries of Richmond County. In addition to the above, the American Title and Trust Company has many other official maps, field notes and historical proofs covering Staten Island from the early dawn of English Colonial History in America down to the present time.

Many of these archives have never seen the light of publicity. The identity, authenticity and official character of each, however, is apparent upon its face and can be promptly and effectively confirmed.

These invaluable proofs settle once and for all the location of each and every English Crown Grant of lands on Staten Island.

There is not now a single building lot on Staten Island that cannot be located on the original tract of land covered by the English Crown Grant to which as a proposition of law it must look as the original source of its title.

These proofs cover upland, salt meadows, beaches, land between high and low water mark and lands under the sea, bays and rivers, to the bounds and limits of Richmond County.

For the first time since the chaotic conditions following the American Revolution, it should be possible to clear up all old titles to lands on Staten Isand and to properly support every good modern title by establishing it upon the basis of the Original Crown Grant from which it descended. To this definite proposition the American Title and Trust Company in the Dupont Building, Wilmington, Delaware, and the American Title and Security Company of Staten Island, are devoting their best resources.

These two Title Companies are not interested in and devote no time or attention to the regular lines of title searching and guaranteeing done by the Title Guarantee and Trust Company, the Lawyers Title and Trust Company, and the New York Title and Mortgage Company of New York City, all so ably and efficiently represented on Staten Island.

These two American Title Companies are, however, preparing and are able to prove the Crown Grant basis to any and all titles to lands on Staten Island where the source of present titles cannot be traced by any Title Company to its original Crown Grant.

This information will remedy the defects which for more than a century have harassed property holders on Staten Island and caused title searching to fall short of perfecting complete chains of title extending back to their true and legitimate fountain head, the English Crown Grants.

The well-informed public deplores the issuance of thousands of restricted and conditional policies of so-called title insurance to home seekers and house builders who may have taken defective titles for building lots under the delusion that they were receiving a complete and perfect policy of title insurance.

A policy of title insurance is adversely affected by each "exception" endorsed on its back and in a multitude of instances is rendered absolutely valueless thereby.

Among the many "exceptions" noted on the back of policies of title insurance issued by the thousands on Staten Island is one which reads substantially as follows:

"This title is not insured as against any facts "which may be disclosed upon an accurate or "correct survey," or words to that effect.

Without intending to impugn any motives but giving full credit to the caution which presumably directs the policy of conservative title companies, we ask one pertinent question:

> If a "correct survey" should disclose the "fact" that the land covered by the policy is on the Symes Grant, then under the terms of the policy the insurance would be void, would it not?

A Title Guarantee Company is only justified in writing a policy consistent with the risk it assumes. It must in the very nature of things disavow liability against what to it is the absolutely unknown danger which clearly threatens it. *The horror of it is,* however, *that innocent purchasers are not informed* by many sellers of real estate as to the limitations hidden away in the terms of such title insurance policies. Serious risks are oft-times actually assumed and unquestionably carried by the one who innocently thinks that the title to his home is fully and completely insured, and for which he pays his hard-earned wages.

To what extent a Title Company is bound in morals to explain to its client the true meaning in the restrictions on the back of its title insurance policies is not for us to determine.

We have been furthermore creditably informed by one who claims to have been a party to the conversation, that thousands of dead are being buried on Staten Island lands the present title record to which lands is held by a corporation, one of the chief officers of which stated that the Company owning the same could not satisfactorily trace back its title.

It is a ghastly statement and worthy of a Ghoul!

To betray the poor and innocent and to mislead them into accepting defective titles and paying their money for the same is inhuman, but for private gain to knowingly, wilfully and deceitfully involve the burial place of the dead should place the guilty beyond the pale of human association!

> "Such, if admitted, would of high heaven a "hades make."

The American Title and Trust Company recently examined a deed given to a home seeker on Staten Island by a so-called Realty Company. The deed was drawn in such a manner as to be of absolutely no value to him in the form delivered. This was no act of a Title Company, but of an alleged Realty Company which had accepted his money and left him in a desperate position as to the actual title to the lands which he had presumably purchased.

The American Title and Trust Company exposed the fraud and offered to bring to Bar without costs to the victim the perpetrator thereof, if the transaction was not forthwith remedied, which was promptly done.

But why do not Title Insurance Companies make a general business of unqualifiedly guaranteeing the title to and peaceable possession of dock properties in Manhattan, Brooklyn, Jersey City, Hoboken, Staten Island and elsewhere on tidal waters?

The explanation if made in full would be beyond the scope and limits of this work. In brief, the State controls and regulates commerce and the waters of the harbors are free.

The lands under water and between high and low

water mark on tidal streams are subject to private ownership, but the State wisely and happily has the power to designate where docks may and may not be built, so as not to interfere with reasonable navigation of the waters.   It may regulate their length, width and form.   It can prescribe of what they shall be constructed and their distance apart.

These are rights inherent in the State for the regulation of commerce and for public safety.   Harbor regulations may change from time to time as the interests of commerce may dictate.

Hence to unqualifiedly warrant a quiet and peaceable possession of lands subject to a Governmental regulation which may and does limit and control the occupancy thereof and the use to which it may be put is impracticable.

Notwithstanding this fact, among the most valuable lands in a city, we find its shore fronts.   Among the safest investments we find dock bonds.

No clearer, cleaner or straighter descent of title to lands can be found than the dock fronts and shore fronts of Staten Island, the Governmental regulation of which is an unmixed blessing to all.

ANALYSIS

OF

ONE OF THE CROWN GRANTS.

English Crown Grant to Lancaster Symes

of

Lands on Staten Island, New York City.

"ANNE BY THE GRACE OF GOD, OF
"GREAT BRITTAIN, FRANCE, IRE-
"LAND, QUEEN, DEFENDER OF THE
"FAITH."

"She was certainly one of the best and most
"unblemished Sovereigns that ever sat upon the
"throne of England and well deserved the ex-
"pressive though simple epithet of 'Good
"Queen Anne.'" (Smollett, History of England, Vol. 3, p. 311; The Major and The
Queen, pp. 28, 29.)

"TO ALL TO WHOM THESE PRESENTS
"SHALL COME, OR MAY CONCERN,
"SENDETH GREETINGS"—

This was not only notice to her realm but to all the world at large.

"WHEN AS OUR LOVING SUBJECT, LAN- "CASTER SYMES, BY HIS PETITION "PRESENTED TO"—

A Royal Grant when couched in strict legal language must always be construed favorably for the Crown and unfavorably for the subject, when uncertainty of language or expression obscures or renders doubtful its exact meaning.

When the Grantor, the Crown, used the term *"our loving subject"* it was always intended to clearly indicate that the Crown knew that it was dealing with a true, faithful and affectionate subject and by the use of that term indicated that the consideration due such an one should at all times be accorded to him. The conditions of the Grant were to be interpreted in the terms of loving consideration for him who was so highly regarded by the Sovereign.

"OUR RIGHT TRUSTY AND WELL-BE- LOVED COUZIN, EDWARD, VISCT CORNBURY CAPT. GENLL AND GOV.R IN CHIEFE OF THE PROVINCE OF NEW YORK AND TERRITORIES DE- PENDING THEREON IN AMERICA AND VICE ADMIRALL OF THE SAME &C IN COUNSELL"—

Queen Anne and Lord Cornbury were cousins. Lancaster Symes was held in very high per-

sonal regard by the Queen and was Lord Cornbury's most intimate and truest personal friend.
For particulars as to the happy relationship and
friendship existing between this trio see "The
Major and the Queen," pages 38, 39.

"HATH PRAYED OUR GRANT AND CON-FIRMATION FOR ALL AND ANY THE PIECES AND PARCELLS OF VACANT AND UNAPPROPRIATED LAND AND MEADOW"—

"The vacant and unappropriated land" of
the realm was distinctively and admittedly the
property of the Crown and could be granted by
it under English common law. Staten Island
lands were also vested in the Crown as personal
Crown lands, by right of private purchase from
the Indians, by the Duke of York.

"ON STATEN ISLAND IN THE COUNTY OF RICHMOND, THE WHICH PETITION WEE BEING WILLING TO GRANT,"—

In a legal sense, an island is never legally
defined in the school book description as "a body
of land surrounded by water." The law does
not recognize any proprietorship in water.
Water may or may not be present on the land.
Staten Island extends by legal definition, to the
bounds and limits of Richmond County.

"Richmond (County) which comprehends
the whole of Staten Island." (Gov. Tryons
Report to the English Crown.)

The Grant made of Manhattan Island was for the vacant and unappropriated land "on Manhattan Island," which carried with it much of the bed of the East River. No notice was taken therein of the latter being submerged land.

In ejectment to recover submerged lands in the Great South Bay, the Bay was described as being *"ON"* the south side of the Island, formerly called Long Island."

The water was not referred to, but the bottom of the Bay was held to have been conveyed.

The Grant of land *ON* Manhattan Island included land under water in the East River.

The Grant of land *ON* the South side of Long Island included the lands under water in the Great South Bay.

The Grant of land *ON* Staten Island included the lands under water "to the bounds and limits of Richmond County."

Sand Bay was officially described in Colonial days as *"ON* Staten Island." (1712.) Sand Bay was again officially described as *"ON* the Eastermost part of Staten Island." (1713.) A Bay is not upland and yet it is *ON* Staten Island.

"Etymologically ON and UPON differ in meaning." (Webster.)

This Grant does not limit its conveyance to lands *UPON* Staten Island, but to lands *ON* Staten Island.

Your coat is ON you when it enwraps your form.

The barnacles are ON the hull of the ship, whether attached to its sides or bottom.

The ring is ON when it encircles the finger.

"In a position, state or *adherance*. In such a position as to cover, *surround* or overspread." (Webster.)

"KNOW YEE THAT OF OUR ESPECIAL GRACE"—

The term "especial grace" can only be comprehended in the light of the true meaning of the English word "Grace." It carries "wealth of an exalted and noble love." Students of English Common Law fully understand that a Crown Grant made out of the most exalted impulse of the soul, to a "loving subject" does not legally carry narrowness of interpretation but on the contrary a full, free and generous construction.

This is clearly stated in Blackstone's Commentaries and in the within chapter "The New World and Crown Grants."

"CERTAIN KNOWLEDGE"—

The expression "certain knowledge" is the Crown's voluntary and gracious way of relieving the applicant of all possible charge of having misrepresented the facts. It was as if the Sovereign said to the world, "I do not wish to hear a word about or against this application

or applicant.   I know all about it and him.   I
have positive and sure information."

"AND MEER MOTION"—

"Meer motion," in other words it would
properly read, "off hand."   It is as if the Crown
had said, "Did my loving subject for whom I
have such a deep and pure affection petition for
these lands and rights?   I Grant them with the
'wave of a hand.'"

"WEE HAVE GIVEN, GRANTED, RATIFIED AND CONFIRMED AND IN AND BY THESE PRESENTS DOE FOR US OUR HEIRS AND SUCCESSORS, GIVE, GRANT, RATIFYE AND CONFIRME UNTO THE SAID LANCASTER SYMES, HIS HEIRS AND ASSIGNS FOREVER."

The Grant was made by the Crown to Lancaster
Symes in behalf of,—

First: The Crown.
Second: The "heirs" of the Crown.   The Duke
         of York had purchased Staten Island.
         It became annexed to the Crown's pri-
         vate Manor of East Greenwich in the
         County of Kent, England.   The Crown
         had children who were heirs of the
         blood or body.   Hence the Crown in
         view of its personal proprietorship of
         Staten Island bound its "heirs" to the

Grant to Lancaster Symes. By this the Crown admitted its personal title.

Third: The Crown bound its "successors" on the throne. This was notice to the world that no Royal successor on the throne of England should ever reassert a claim to the lands granted by the Queen of England, but especially by the Lady of the Monor of East Greenwich. This provision estoppes the State of New York.

It was in effect a Grant by the Lady of the Manor of a part of her manorial estate, which Grant was confirmed by the Crown, the Sovereign acting in a dual capacity. The Great Seal of the Province was a ratification by the people.

The State of New York subsequently confirmed this Grant.

The Grant was not simply a life tenure to Symes, but was a Grant of title to him and his "heirs and assigns *forever.*"

"ALL THE BEFORE MENCONED PIECES AND PARCELLS OF VACANT AND UN-APPROPRIATED LAND AND PREMISES AND ALL AND SINGULAR THE HEREDITAMENTS AND APPUTE-NANCES THEREUNTO BELONGING."

"The vacant and unappropriated lands" on Staten Island belonged to the Crown (Uplands, lands between high and low water mark, and lands under water to the bounds and limits of Richmond County). They were not only granted, but the hereditaments and appurtenances also "belonging" thereto.

First: "The hereditaments" — "Things capable of being inherited."

Second: "The appurtenances" — "Everything passes which is necessary to the full enjoyment thereof and *which is in use as incident or appurtenant thereto.*"

"WITHIN THE BOUNDS AND LIMITS ABOVE IN THESE PRESENTS MENCONED AND EXPRESSED."

This is a clear reference to the hereinbefore set forth expression "in the County of Richmond." Legally there is no difference in force and effect between "on Staten Island" and "in the County of Richmond." The two are interchangeable terms,—the County of Richmond and Staten Island being legally co-extensive and with common boundaries. Staten Island represents *the land,* the County of Richmond the local governmental *jurisdiction thereover.* One is material the other is political and governmental. They are co-extensive.

"TOGETHER WITH ALL AND SINGULAR, THE WOODS, UNDERWOODS, TREES, TIMBER, FEEDINGS, MEADOWS,

MASHES, SWAMPS, POOLES, PONDS,
WATERS, WATERCOURSES, RIVERS,
RIVOLETTS, RUNS AND STREAMS OF
W A T E R , BROOKS, FFISHING AND
FFOWLING, H U N T I N G , HAWKING,
MINES AND MINERALLS, STANDING,
GROWING LYEING, OR BEING OR TO
BE HAD"—

The Crown further granted "together with
all and singular the

"woods, underwoods,"

> According to Lord Coke, "a grant to an-
> other of all his woods will pass not only
> all his trees but the land on which they
> grow."

"trees,"

> Trees are a part of the real estate, while
> growing and before they are severed from
> the freehold. When they are cut down
> they become personal property.

"timber,"

> Timber trees are those used in building
> and in mechanical arts. Timber trees con-
> stitute a portion of the realty.

"ffeedings,"

> These are pasturing lands where cattle and

herds may graze and from which fodder may be cut and taken.

"meadows,"

These consist of low ground adjacent to streams, tracts of low or level land, producing grass which is mowed for hay; cultivated land, growing grass sowed thereon; tillable, mowing or grass land. The term is applied to the tracts which lie above the shore and are or may be overflowed by spring and extraordinary tides only and yield grasses which are good for hay.

"mashes,"

In this word the English Crown "dropped its r." Mashes are low and wet ground, much if not all of the time being overflowed by water.

"swamps,"

Low lying land covered more or less with water,—bogs.

"pooles,"

A small lake of standing water. "By the grant of a pool, both the land and the water will pass. Undoubtedly the right to fish will be acquired by such a grant."

"ponds," "pools," "waters,"

> A pool of water or a stream of water is considered as part of the land. A mere grant of water passes a fishery.

"watercourses,"

> This term is applied to the flow or movement of the water in rivers, creeks, and other streams.
> "In a legal sense property in a water course is comprehended under the general name of land." (Bouvier—"watercourse.")

"rivers,"

> A natural stream of water flowing between banks. The only rivers within the "bounds and limits of Richmond County" are the Hudson, Kill von Kull, Arthur Kill and Raritan Bay, which is the confluent of the three rivers.

"rivoletts," "runs and streams of water, "brooks,"

> This description comprehends every stream of running water "in the County of Richmond."

"ffishing,"

> By the common law of England the fisheries in all the navigable waters of the

realm belonged to the Crown. "An individual claiming an exclusive fishery in such waters must show it by Grant or Prescription."

"fowling, hunting, hawking,"

These rights and privileges theretofore possessed by the Crown as a Royal prerogative or as the private owner under manorial rights were conveyed by the Crown to Lancaster Symes.

"mines and minerals,"

Gold and silver mines (as later referred to herein) were held under the common law of England as Royal mines and belonged to the Crown. It was an open question where mines, producing minerals of the baser sort, contained mixed in such ore, gold or silver of a value equal to or exceeding the value of the baser metals, whether the same were not of Royal value and belonged to the Crown. To remedy this uncertainty laws were passed by Parliament (in the Statutes I William and Mary st I, c 30, and 8 w. and M., c. 6). Under these Statutes the usual gold bearing ores,—copper, tin, lead and iron, were exempt from all claims by the Crown as Royal mines and as its exclusive property on condition, however, that the King should have the right to purchase such products of the mines at prices

stated in the act.   This provision made by
Parliament was accepted by Crown and
people as just and equitable.

The "mines and minerals" on Staten
Island were owned by the Crown through
the purchase thereof by the Duke of York.
Under the Grant to Lancaster Symes the
Crown conveyed to him all mining rights,
excepting those of gold and silver, in the
lands conveyed under the said Grant.   Le-
gend has it, though sharply testing human
credulity, that some gold was at one time
mined on Staten Island near Richmond.
Considerable iron ore, large quantities of
clay for making brick, and a certain grade
of kaolin have been mined on Staten Island.

"standing, growing, lyeing, or being or to be
"had,"

This term covered and included timber and
trees together with any and all of the aforesaid natural growths and earth deposits
therein contained or existing thereon.

"USED AND ENJOYED IN THEM THE BOUNDS AND LIMITS AFORESAID."

This provision specifically grants all rights of
use and enjoyment at the time possessed by the
Crown within "the bounds and limitts" of Richmond County.   The Crown had thereinbefore
granted the title to the described lands and in
this latter clause of the Grant gave to the

Grantee the use and enjoyment thereof to the bounds and limits of Richmond County

(a) of every class of timbered growth thereon.

(b) of all agricultural soil thereon.

(c) of all lands thereon of a marshy nature, towit: occasionly submerged lands, semi-submerged lands on which vegetation grows and appears above the surface of the water

(d) of all pools with unknown outlets, ponds of like character or with outlets. Lakes of every kind and character which are comprehended in the foregoing, in brooks that run, rivolets that flow, rivers that course their way, water-courses, the characteristics of which are included in the name thereof. Then lacking descriptive power as to further details the comprehensive words are added "runs and streams of water." All such are to be "used and enjoyed" by the Grantee, his heirs and assigns forever. The sporting strain in the English blood is further evidenced by the additional Grant of the fishing (which legally includes shell and swimming fish) rights, fowling rights and hunting rights, on all classes of land referred to and on and in the standing, running, flowing and tidal waters legally included in the Encyclopedically described waters. But where are all these rights and privileges to be enjoyed and to what bounds do the lands and waters extend? The Grant says "In them the bounds and limits aforesaid." The ultra-narrow constructionist who, legally unadvised might say "on Staten Island" would overlook the words "in them the bounds and limits aforesaid." The possibility of such a construction absolutely disappears in face of the fact that the County of Richmond referred to therein had been delimited and its boundaries fixed by Statute.

That the Grant was intended to cover all lands under water in Richmond County is clear when we remember that the bounds and limits of Staten Island at every point are in the Rivers and to reach the bounds and limits the lands must of necessity extend at every point under water.

The word *ON* as it appears in the term "on Staten Island," has been exhaustively commented on in this chapter.

"AND ALL OTHER PROFITTS, BENEFITTS, ADVANTAGES, HEREDITAMENTS AND APPURTENANCES WHATSO-EVER UNTO THE SD PEICES AND PARCELLS OF LAND AND PREMISES

BELONGING OR IN ANY WISE APPUR-
TEYING (EXCEPT AND ALWAYS RE-
SERVED OUT OF THIS OUR PRESENT
G R A N T ALL GOLD AND SILVER
MINES)."

It would appear that the rights and powers
granted therein by the Crown, prior to this latter clause were sufficiently couched in broadest
language. It, however, adds "all other profits,
benefits, advantages, hereditaments and appurtenances whatsoever."   The Crown fearing
that even that term might lack sufficiency then
added, "in any wise appurtaining."

(We note the exception of "gold and silver
mines therefrom.)

"TO HAVE AND TO HOLD THE SAID
PEICES AND PARCELLS OF LAND
AND PREMISES WITH THEIR APPUR-
TENANCES HEREBY GRANTED MEN-
CONED OR INTENDED TO BE HERE-
BY GRANTED AS AFORSAID (EXCEPT
BEFORE EXCEPTED) UNTO THE SAID
LANCASTER SYMES, HIS HEIRS AND
ASSIGNS FOREVER TO THE ONLY
PROPER USE AND BEHOOF OF THE
SD LANCASTER SYMES HIS HEIRS
AND ASSIGNS FOREVER."

This paragraph in the light of the preceding
terms needs no additional comment, excepting
however that a broad and generous construction
is required to be placed upon this Grant, by the

use of the words "or intended to be hereby granted." The Crown then suddenly puts a final and arbitrary restriction upon the exercise of the rights and privileges hereinbefore described, by absolutely limiting the same "to the only proper use and behoofe of the said Lancaster Symes his heirs and assigns forever."

"TO BE HOLDIN OF US OUR HEIRS AND SUCCESSORS IN FFREE AND COMMON SOCCAGE."

The Crown Grants to lands on Staten Island provided that the title to such lands should be held "in free and common soccage." Some authorities claim that this word is derived from the old Saxon word "soke," meaning a "Ploughshare." If so, it signifies that the Grantee who received a Grant of land from the Crown obtained his title under the condition that he would perform certain (or sure) services; hence the legal maxim, "Soccage is the same as service of the plough."

Pel. Leg. Max.—also Coke Litt. 86a.

Blackstone and others have held that the word "soccage" is derived from the word "soc," which meant "free" or "privileged." This conclusion is consistent with the fact that any one who held "title in soccage" under a Crown Grant, while required to perform certain or definite services to the Crown as a consideration for holding such title, was not required under the terms of the Grant to perform military service.

The meaning of the term, therefore as used in the Staten Island Crown Grants is that the Grantees, as long as they held title to their lands, were required to perform the definite services provided for in the Grants, free from military duty. The failure of such performance permitted re-entry upon and re-possession of the land by the Crown.

In the year 1830, the State of New York, by special enactment, prohibited any further issue of any Grants of lands in the State of New York, the tenure of which was to be held on a soccage basis.

"AS OF OUR MANOR OF EAST GREEN-
WICH IN THE COUNTY OF KENT
WITHIN THE REALME OF ENGLAND
YEILDING, RENDRING AND PAYING
THEREFORE YEARLY AND EVERY
YEAR FROM HENCEFORTH FOREVER
UNTO US OUR HEIRS AND SUCCES-
SORS ATT OUR CUSTOME HOUSE ATT
NEW YORKE TO OUR COLLER RE-
CEIVR GENLL THEREFORE THE
TIME BEING ATT OR UPON THE
FEAST DAY OF THE ANNUNCIATION
OF OUR BLESSED VIRGIN MARY
(COMMONLY CALLED LADY DAY)
THE RENT OR SUME OF SIX SHILL-
INGS CEINT MONEY OF NEW YORK
IN LIEU AND STEAD OF ALL OTHER

RENTS, DUTYS, SERVICES, DUES AND DEMANDS WHATSOEVER."

We now find that while the Grant conveyed all the Crown's title, rights and privileges (excepting gold and silver mining), the Grant has a dual character. That is—the Crown acted in a dual capacity. The Queen made the Grant with all her Royal authority but the same person, Anne, Lady of the Manor of East Greenwich, to which Manor Staten Island was attached, made the Grant as from that Manor and required that the accounting should be made through the New York Custom House to the Manor House in East Greenwich in the County of Kent, England.

(See Chapter herein entitled "Manor of East Greenwich and Crown Grants.")

"IN TESTIMONY WHEREON WEE HAVE CAUSED THESE OUR LETTERS TO BE MADE PATTENTS AND THE SEALE OF OUR SAID PROVINCE OF NEW YORK TO OUR SD LETTERS, PATTENTS TO BE AFFIXED AND THE SAME TO BE RECORDED IN TH SECRYR OF OUR SAID PROVINCE.

WITNESS OUR RIGHT, TRUSTY AND WELL BELOVED COUZIN EDWD VISCOT CORNBURY CAPT GENLL & GOVR IN CHIEFE IN AND OUT THEREON PROVINCE OF NEW YORK AFORESD

AND TERRITORIES DEPENDING
THEREON IN AMERICA AND VICE
ADMIRAL OF THE SAME &C. IN
COUNSEL ATT OUR OWN FORT ATT
NEW YORK THE TWENTY SEVENTH
DAY OF OCTOBER IN THE SEVENTH
YEAR OF OUR REIGN ANNY DOMINI,
1708."

The Royal Seal carved in hard wood was pendant from the Grant.

The Seal of the Province of New York was also attached to the Grant.

"Words are not to be looked at so much as
"the cause and nature of the thing, since the
"intention of the contracting parties may appear
"from those rather than from words."
(Calvinus Lex.)

"It seems, however, the provisions of Colo-
"nial charters are to be liberally construed,
"whenever necessary to accomplish the pur-
"pose of the Grant."
(Delancey vs. Piepgras, 138 N. Y., 26.)

"English political economy and English popu-
"lar notions are very deeply and extensively
"pervaded by the assumption that all property
"has been acquired through an original trans-
"action of purchase and that *whatever be the*
"*disadvantages of the form it takes they were*
"*nal sale.*"
"*allowed for in the consideration for the origi-*

(Maine, Early Laws and Customs, page 325.)

"By coming to the Crown they became grantable in that way to the subject."

(Burke, Dormant Claims of the Church.)

QUIT RENTS

AND

CROWN GRANTS

The King's Grants were matters of public record. No freehold may be given to a King, nor derived from him but by matter of record. All Grants made by the King must first pass through the hands of several regular subordinate officers appointed for that purpose whose duty it was to transcribe and enroll the same. The paramount duty of these subordinate officers is to closely examine and inspect the form, nature and character of such Grants and to inform the King if anything contained therein is improper or unlawful to be granted. Such Grants are contained in charters or letters patent, that is, open letters. They are so called, because they are not sealed up, but are exposed to open view, with the Great Seal pending at the bottom, and are usually directed or addressed by the King to all his subjects at large.

A Grant or letters patent must first pass by Bill, prepared by the Attorney General, pursuant to a warrant from the Crown. It is then subscribed at the top, with the King's own sign manual and sealed with his privy-signet, which is always held in the custody of the principal Secretary of State. At times, Grants immediately pass under the Great Seal, in which case the patent is subscribed in the following words. "Per Ipsum Regem," by the King himself. Certain Grants of minor importance are issued with less ceremony, but always with care, caution and circumspection.

A Crown Grant issued at the petition of the Grantee, is construed most favorably for the Crown and against the Grantee, whereas a Grant made by a subject to another citizen, is construed strongly against the Grantor.

To overcome this legal presumption in favor of the Crown as against the Grantee, the Crown at times adopted a phrase asserting the exercise "of special Grace," "certain knowledge" and "mere motion" on the part of the Crown. In making a Grant expressing clemency, generosity and good will on the part of *the Crown toward the Grantee, the Crown imparted to the construction of the Grant a liberal and* generous interpretation in behalf of the Grantee.

(The foregoing paragraph condensed and adopted from Blackstone, Vol. 2, pages 346, 347.)

The gracious attitude of Queen Anne towards Lancaster Symes is evidenced in the final Grant of lands on Staten Island, made to him by the Crown, as indicated in the following expressions from the Crown Grant issued to him:

"Our loving subject Lancaster Symes,"—"Know "yee that of our Especial Grace certain knowl- "edge and meer motion wee have given granted "etc., unto the said Lancaster Symes his heirs "and assigns forever."

This form of language used by the Crown in the Symes Grant gave to it the broadest construction under common law.

Digby, in his History of the Law of Real Property, page 34, states that,

> "by the conquest, King William (of Nor-
> "mandy) succeeded to all of the rights of the
> "Anglo Saxon Kings.   The rights over the
> "land which they had became his."
> "The great possessions *held by them in their*
> "*private capacity* devolved upon William, and
> "*no distinction any longer existed between the*
> "*King's ownership of lands in his private capa-*
> "*city and his suzerainty over the folkland as*
> "*chief of the nation.*"
>
> "ALL ALIKE BECAME 'TERRA REGIS.' "   (KING'S
> "LAND.)

We find in Freeman's "Constitutional History," Vol. 5, page 787:

> "It was necessary at the time of Doomsday, to
> "a good title to any land, except that held by
> "ecclesiastical bodies, that the tenant should be
> "able to adduce evidence of a Grant, re-grant
> "or confirmation by William."

This theory of tracing real estate back to English Crown Grants has been a recognized principle in English Common Law from the time of the "Dooms-day Book" and the same principle became fundamental in America when English Common Law was brought to the Colonies upon the establishment therein of English sovereignty.

It is in accordance with this theory of Common Law, established in England and adopted in America, that all titles to land on Staten Island must find their source in an English Crown Grant.

The Grants made by the English Crown for lands on Staten Island were in fact deeds which passed the title to the Grantee. They were issued subject to the annual payment of quit-rents (meaning quit-the-rents). In the event of non-payment of such rentals, the right of re-entry upon and re-possession of such lands so conveyed was retained and possessed by the English sovereign.

This form of deed is now substantially obsolete in this country. It has been proscribed by nearly all, if not all, of our states.

The quit-rents provided to be paid under the terms of the Staten Island Grants were payable at the Custom House in the City of New York and on account of the rent roll of the Manor of East Greenwich in the County of Kent, England.

This arrangement for the collection of the quit-rents proved to be extremely unsatisfactory. Historians disagree as to the proportion of the rentals collected from Staten Island, which *eventually reached the Manor House* of East Greenwich. Some authorities claim that *"it was as much as twenty per cent."*

In addition to the difficulties, incident to distance, connected with the collection of quit-rents, unbusinesslike methods on the part of the Grantees predominated.   Many of them defaulted in payments, much of the lands granted were abandoned by the Grantees without notice to the Crown.   Others of the Grants were not recorded, while a number of them were not patented.

The official records clearly show that many of the Grantees applied for their Grants, and upon securing the issue thereof, failed to record the same. Others recorded their Grants but paid no quit-rents. There were other Grants applied for, issued, but were not confirmed.   We even find at this day modern titles claiming unconfirmed Grants and unpatented lands as a source from which their so-called rights descend.

"In the absence of a statute, a ground rent is not within any statute of limitations nor is there any presumption that it has ceased to exist from the mere lapse of time without payment of the rent or from mere delay of the owner of the ground rent in demanding it."   (20 Cyc. 1379.)

It has been held that in the event of the non-payment of quit-rents for a period of twenty years, and no demand having been made by the Grantor for such payment within said consecutive years the Court will presume that such quit-rents have been paid, but proof to the contrary is admissable.   Such attitude of the Court will in no wise release the Grantee from the payment of prior quit-rents which remain unpaid.   *The non-payment of quit-rents for a period of twenty years does not give adverse possession to the title as against the Grantor.*   Any and all parties *laying claim to title under a Grant conveying such title subject to a quit-rent* (which runs with the land) *cannot claim adverse possession* against the Grantor nor be relieved from liability to pay such quit-rents except by act of the Grantor. Any Grants made subsequent to 1830 and subject to quit-rents are void in the State of New York, by special enactment of the State Legislature. Crown Grants made prior thereto are unaffected thereby.

In the years from 1814 to 1816 inclusive there were several acts passed by the New York Legislature contemplating and providing for the commutation of quit-rents then due or to become payable to the State. Such commutation was to be conditioned upon election on the part of the Grantees to commute the same. Pursuant thereto, the quit-rents under the Crown Grant to Lancaster Symes were commuted and paid in full forever, as is shown in the records of the Comptroller's office at Albany.

"The effect of the commutation of the quit-rents is the same upon the rights of the parties as if the people had made a new grant of the patent without reservation."

(People vs. Renssellaer, 9 N. Y., 291, 328.)

"People may not bring ejectment after commuting quit-rents."

(People vs. van Renssellaer, 9 N. Y., 292.)

Under this and like decisions the State of New York representing the people, has no standing in the Courts upon which it could base an action for the nullification or cancellation of the English Crown

Grant to Lancaster Symes.   It has evidenced no disposition so to do, and is barred from pleading that the Crown Grant to Lancaster Symes is null and void.

On the contrary, the State of New York has admitted the Grant and denied title to any land in itself on Staten Island.

MANOR OF EAST GREENWICH

AND

CROWN GRANTS

Students of American Colonial History have been much interested in the fact that substantially all of the English Colonial charters have not been directly issued "as of" the English Crown. In nearly all such charters it is provided that while the land so granted is to be held as from the Crown of England it is, however, to be held "as of the Manor of East Greenwich in the County of Kent, in free and common soccage and not *in capite* or of knight service?" It is a pertinent inquiry, "Why should the land granted in the New World, by the English Sovereign be held from some Manor and not from the Crown direct?" Why was it to be held in free and common soccage and not by knight service? Why should the Manor of East Greenwich have been nearly always selected in preference to other Royal Manors?" Above all, the one inquiry is of paramount importance—why should Colonial Charters of various kinds and why should Colonial Grants to lands in America be held as of a Royal Manor or Manors of which the King was "the Lord of the Manor," rather than directly from the Sovereign of England? If there was no legal significance in this arrangement, why were not some of these Grants or Charters held as of Westminster, one of the Crown residences, with its full, complete and efficient administrative force? The answer is:

"Westminster was not a Manor."

The Manor of East Greenwich and Hundred of Blackheath in the County of Kent, England, situated about four miles from London Bridge, embraced among other lands what is now Greenwich, with its Royal Observatory and Naval Hospital. The old palace was known as the "Greenwich House," and was a favorite royal residence as early as 1300 A. D.

The title to the Manor of East Greenwich, with its manorial rights and privileges, has been at times held by various *English Sovereigns as a part or portion of their personal Crown lands* and at other times by Grantees of the Crown *outside of the line of royal descent.*

Henry V granted it to Thomas Beauford, the Duke of Exeter, from whom it passed as a manorial estate to Humphrey the Duke of Gloucester. The latter greatly improved and beautified the property and named it "Placentia." At his death in 1447 it was acquired by the then reigning King and was again added to the Crown's private estate.

In this palace was born Henry VIII. It was the birth place of both Queen Mary and Queen Elizabeth and under its roof King Edward VI died.

The Manor House was enlarged by Edward IV, also by Henry VIII, who made it one of his favorite residences. James I added to it and Charles I erected the "Queen House" adjacent to it for Henrietta Maria.

At the time of the English Revolution the Protector appropriated to his own use this Manor with other personal Crown estates and private palaces of the Crown, but it was returned upon the restoration of Charles II.

Upon the acquisition of this Manor by Charles II, what was left of the historic Manor House with its improvements, was demolished by the King and a building which now constitutes the West wing of the Naval Hospital was erected as one unit of a very elaborate design contemplating a royal residence of great splendor. The plan was not carried out but the building so erected was occasionally used by that King as a residence.

The building so constructed was granted by King William and Queen Mary at the suggestion of the latter, as a royal gift, for a home for disabled sailors of the Royal Navy. It was a personal endowment accompanied by a gift of two thousand pounds from the private purse of the Royal benefactors.

"On the restoration of Charles II in 1660 the Manor (East Greenwich) and those demesnes, undemised by the Crown returned to the *Royal revenue,* part of which the Manor itself, continues at this time." (1886.)

It is now (1917) a part of the personal estate of the English Sovereign from which Grants may even yet be made by the Crown without let or hinderance.

England's great architects such as Inigo Jones, his son-in-law Webb and the immortal Sir Christopher Wren with others here displayed their genius in architecture. Sovereign after Sovereign and others of wealth have here poured out their gifts for the

Men of the Sea.   Englishmen here show with pride
a wonderful group of buildings bearing the names of
many English Sovereigns representing great bene-
factions to the sea defenders of the realm.

Not all of the old Manor of East Greenwich was
included in the Hospital and Observatory Grants.
One interesting prerogative still clings to the English
Sovereigns under their East Greenwich manorial
privileges still retained and held by each as Lord of
this Manor of East Greenwich.   It is the patronage
of the living of St. Marys, the Greenwich Vicarage.
St. Mary's Church is within the bounds of the old
Manor of East Greenwich in the County of Kent.
His English Majesty may be largely an ornamental
Sovereign, useful at social and State functions, but
as Lord of the Manor he yet has absolute power to
appoint the Vicar of St. Mary's Parish.   The Manor
is the property of the King and not of the kingdom
and its benefits inure to the private income of the
English Crown.   The House of Commons may vote
the downfall of the Empire's Ministry, to which the
Sovereign must bow, but the King as Lord of the
Manor has the absolute power to retain or discharge
the Vicar of St. Mary's Parish, before which the
people must bow.

We find that any Grant having been made by the
English Crown covering lands in America, the cus-
tom prevailed in England of making such Grants of
Crown lands as of the Sovereign's Manor.

The rights and powers possessed under the charter
of the Manor of East Greenwich, and exercised by
the Lord or Lady of the Manor, did not differ in any
material or substantial way from the rights and pow-

ers properly exercised by the Lord or Lady of other Manors. There is nothing, therefore, exceptional, unusual or specially significant in the selection of the Manor of East Greenwich in preference to the selection of other Manors, of which the King was the Lord or the Queen was the Lady excepting however that the original Grant of the Duke of York and other basic American Grants were made as of the Manor of East Greenwich.

The peculiar significance in such transactions was in the fact that the Crown in dealing with much of the Crown lands made such Grants "to be held as of the Manor" and not as of the Throne.

"They were Grants by the King and not by the Kingdom." When land was granted it was of the *personal* Crown Estate while political authority when granted was by *kingly prerogative*.

The three Charters of Virginia granted by James I were held as of the Manor of East Greenwich; so was also the New England Charter, issued in 1620; all these were granted by James I, between 1606 and the latter date. Charles I in his Grant of Massachusetts Bay Charter in 1629, and the Charter for the State of Maine in 1639, were held as of the said Manor of East Greenwich. Charles II then followed by issuing the two Charters of the Carolinas in 1663 and 1665, respectively and with the Rhode Island and Providence plantations charter in 1663. The two famous Grants to the Duke of York covering New England, New York and New Jersey, in 1664 and 1674 respectively were likewise held from the King of England, *"as of the Manor of East*

Greenwich in the County of Kent in free and common
soccage and not in capite or by knight service."

Among all the American Colonial Charters, the
only departure in such practice were the Grants of
Maryland, in 1632, and Pennsylvania in 1681, in
each of which it was provided that the same was to
be held of the Manor of Windsor in the County of
Berks, England. That of Georgia, granted in 1732,
was granted as of the Manor of Hampton Court in
the County of Surrey, England.

The issue of Grants of lands to be held as of the
King's Manor and not direct from the Crown, has
profound legal significance. This is best expressed
in the language of an eminent authority as follows:

> "It was simply an adaptation to land beyond
> "the sea, of a form originally used in the grant
> "of Crown lands in England. Its use may be
> "taken to represent the closeness of the legal
> "connection between the colony and the home
> "government—*that America was, in the view*
> "*of the King, simply an extension of the soil*
> "*of England."*

This declaration prepares us for the statement that
the original title to waste, vacant, unappropriated and
unpatented lands of the realm was vested in the
Crown; that the English Sovereign by and with the
assistance of its Council, *which it appointed and*
could ignore, made Grants, therefore, to individuals
and corporate bodies; that lands granted thereunder
were held as of an English Manor, of which the
English Sovereign was Lord or Lady. Therefore
we must hark back to English Common Law pre-

vailing at that time to properly interpret and understand the rights, conditions and stipulations expressed in the Crown Grants so issued. To understand the privileges enjoyed and the obligations incurred under English Crown Grants to lands on Staten Island, we must refer and defer to the Common Law of England then governing the land tenures of the Manor of East Greenwich in the County of Kent.

"The tenures of Kent were conclusive to the "Court when judicially interpreting and defin- "ing the Common Law of England as relating "to land titles."

ADVERSE POSSESSIONS

CROWN GRANTS

If it be true that the original source of every good title was in the one Great Sovereign, and that it has descended from the Beneficent King, for the comfort and well being of his subjects, certainly a title by adverse possession constitutes a complete reversal of that theory and must have emanated from the chief potentate of the nether world.

The feudal system, with all that followed therefrom was based upon military conquest. It constituted the reward of the victor. The victim, however, in flight from his foe, explained to those upon whom his presence had been forced, that his adversary had violently seized his estate and now held it by adverse possession.

Society of even a Christian civilization, appears at times to have found it necessary to accept the obnoxious doctrine that "Might makes right" even though the Furies themselves overwhelm with cruel violence the weak and innocent. A *de facto* tyrannical government, though based on violence and bloodshed is recognized by the family of nations if it sustains itself for a reasonable period even at the expense of human liberty and freedom.

A nation seizing and holding territory by conquest

in an unrighteous war, extends its jurisdiction and thereafter receives international approval and recognition of its sovereignty so unrighteously obtained if it but maintains possession and stamps into submission its newly but murderously acquired province.

Adverse possession is the child of this unholy doctrine but is accorded recognition in the temple of Justice, but under rigid surveillance of the law. We are not, therefore, surprised to find it looked upon in our legal text-books as a foe of human society, and yet as deemed a "necessary evil." It quiets litigation after maintaining a hostile grip upon properties not its own until such evil possession "ripens into a possessary title."

> "There are cases where title by Adverse Pos-
> "session may, and will, be upheld. *If there is*
> *"no disputed question of fact,* and the posses-
> "session has been clearly adverse and undis-
> "turbed for the required period, the title *may be*
> "sustained. But even in such a case *that class*
> *"of titles is not looked upon with much favor*
> *"by persons who contemplate purchasing the*
> *"property or loaning their money thereon or by*
> *"the Courts."*

> (Harley vs. James, 50 N. Y., 38.)
> (Heller vs. Cohen, 154 N. Y., 299.)

"There are five essential elements necessary to "constitute effective adverse possession:"

"First: The possession must be hostile and
               under a claim of right.

"Second: It must be actual.
"Third: It must be open and notorious.
"Fourth: It must be exclusive.
"Fifth: It must be continuous.

"If any of these constituants is wanting, the pos-
"session will not effect a bar of the legal title."
(Enc. of Law, 2nd Ed., 795.)

"A claim to land, unaccompanied by actual pos-
"session will not ripen into a title, however long and
"persistently such claim is asserted."
(Cyl. of Law & P., Vol. I, 983.)

"A residence in the vicinity of the land, and a
claim to it, though such claim is generally recognized
and spoken of in the neighborhood and affirmed by
the vicinage, unaccompanied by any of the acts and
inditia of ownership, is insufficient to constitute ownership."
(Wood vs. McGuire, 15 Ga., 202.)

"The acts relied upon to establish adverse posses-
"sion must always be as distinct as the character of
"the land reasonably admits of, and must be exer-
"cised with sufficient continuity to acquaint the owner,
"should he visit the land, with the fact that a claim of
"ownership adverse to his title is being asserted.
"Trivial and disconnected acts, doubtful and equivo-
"cal in their character, and which do not clearly
"indicate the intention with which they are per-
"formed, cannot be regarded as amounting to
"possession.   Otherwise a man might be disseized

"without his knowledge and the statutes of limita-
"tions might run against him while he had no ground
"to believe that his seizen had been interrupted."
(Cyl. of L. & P. Vol. I, 985.)

"Where adverse possession is sought to be shown
"by an enclosure of the land for the length of time
"prescribed in the statutes, such an enclosure must be
"a real and substantial one."

"The land must be completely enclosed."

"Land fenced only on two sides, one of the other
"sides abutting upon an unfenced highway and in-
"dicated only by marked trees, is not protected by
"a substantial enclosure."   (Pope vs. Hanmer, 59
Am. Dec. 115.)

"The fencing of three sides of an oblong or square
"piece of land is not a sufficient enclosure to make an
"adverse possession so as to vest title in a wrong-
"doer as against the real owner, though such fences
"exclude the latter from the use and enjoyment of
"the land."   (Armstrong vs. Risteau, 59 Am. Dec.
115.)

"Placing a fence consisting of small posts with two
"rails nailed on around a piece of land, without
"actually occupying the land or any part of it, and
"suffering the fence to go to decay in a year or two
"so that it will not keep out cattle, is not sufficient to
"constitute prima facia evidence of title to the land
"by actual possession.'   (Borel vs. Rollins 20 Cal.
408.)

"A fence which the owner attempts to keep in re-

"pair constitutes an actual enclosure for the purpose
"of adverse possession, though a plank is sometimes
"off or a plank down." (44 S. W. 111.)

"The enclosure alone is not sufficient. It must be
"attended by actual possession."

"The payment of taxes upon land does not con-
"stitute actual possession of it." (Ambrose Oreg.
484, 56, Pac. 513.)

"Surveying the land, maping the same, and issu-
"ing a mortgage thereon, and occasionally entering
"upon the land to look after it, employing an agent
"so to do, or to occasionally cut and carry off fire-
"wood and rails therefrom, does not constitute actual
"possession." (Cyl. L. & P. Vol. I, 993.)

"The fact that the claimant of land posts notices
"upon it merely indicates an intention to hold the
"land, and is not sufficient proof of adverse possess-
"ion." (Lynde vs. Williams 68 Mo. 360.)

"The fact that one claiming a large tract of land
"under a deed, sold and conveyed many small tracts
"within the boundary is insufficient to show actual
"possession; so is the fact that the claimant offered
"the whole tract for sale and listed it for taxation."
(Fuller vs. Elizabeth City 23 S. E. 922.)

In the case of Jackson vs. Bonnell (9 Johns 163)
The Court held as to adverse possession, "The doc-
"trine of the Court with respect to adverse posses-
"sion is that it is to be taken strictly and not to be
"made out by inference but by clear and positive
"proof. *Every presumption is in favor of possess-*

"ion in subordination to the title of the true owner."

In the case of Robers vs. Baumgarten (110 N. Y.) the Court held: "Proof of an occasional resort "to the lands in question in the cutting of salt meadow "grass would not be sufficient to establish occupancy "or possession in the absence of a deed describing and "including them."

In the case of the Mission of the Immaculate Virgin vs. Cronin (143 N. Y. 524), the Court found that: "Where land is unenclosed, uncultivated and "unoccupied, the fact that a person has for twenty "years claimed title thereto, surveyed it, marked its "boundaries by monuments, cut trees thereon from "time to time, and for a few years has paid taxes "thereon, do not establish adverse possession; nor "do these facts, in the absence of constructive or ac- "tual possession authorize the presumption of a Grant "from the true owner." (Distinguishing Roe vs. Strong, 119 N. Y. 316.) (Williams vs. Rand 9 Tex. Civ. App. 651.)

In the case of McRoberts vs. Bergman (132 N. Y. 73) in which case *Bergman relied upon adverse possession and refused to stand upon a deed which he claimed to have,* showing title descending to him *from Lancaster Symes,* the Court held that the "plaintiff must recover upon the strength of his own title and not upon the weakness of that of the defendant. Where the former shows a title better in respect to his right of possession, he is entitled to recover."

Nowhere in the report of this case is the Lancaster Symes Grant referred to or his name introduced by the Court or by the Counsel for either plaintiff or defendant.

The Symes Grant was not at issue in this case despite the frequently and much quoted legal tradition that such was the case.

"A party cannot claim by adverse possession against the State if he took under a conveyance recognizing the public right." (Bridge vs. Wyckoff, 67 N. Y. 130.)

No one having accepted a Grant from the State can successfully claim thereunder as against the true owner where the title claimed by the State has failed.

"A Crown patent is conclusive as against a title "founded on mere adverse occupancy or those wrong- "fully in possession." Gibson vs. Choteau 113 Wall 92; Parmelee vs. Oswega S. Co. 6 N. Y. 74.)

Constructive possession was sufficient under English Common Law.

"A party out of actual possession but who is in "constructive possession may bring action for tres- "pass." (Smith vs. Milles. Burnford & East Rep. Vol. I, 475, Court of Kings Bench, 1786.)

"Silence is not a bar to a later assertion of title." (Thompson vs. Simpson 128 N. Y. 270.)

"No title to land under water can be acquired as "against the State or its Grantee by planting oysters "thereon for any length of time without other title "than that so sought to be acquired." (People vs. Lowndes 55 Hun., N. Y. 469 8 N. Y. Suppl. 908.)

"From the nature of the property it is difficult to "show such a possession of land under water as is "required to support the presumption of a Grant; "as *we fail to find any case* where anything short of "a permanent and exclusive occupation of the soil has "been granted as sufficient." (Boswell on Lim. and Ad. Possessions.)

"The permission or command of the State can give "no power to convey private rights even for a public "service without payment of compensation." (Muhlker vs. N. Y. & R. Co. 197 U. S. 544. Birrell vs. N. Y. & R. Co. 198 U. S. 390. Siegel vs. N. Y. & R. Co. 200 U. S. 615.)

"One may not improve another's land without his "consent and charge him therefor." (Spruck vs. McRoberts 139 N. Y. 193.)

"Docks and two marine railways were not suffi- *"cient to establish adverse possession on the shore-* *"front."* (Delancey vs. Piepgrass 138 N. Y. 26.)

"The owner of the uplands had continued his "boundary fences to low water mark, to prevent cat- "tle passing around them, and had built a bulkhead "and filled in with earth a small portion of the land "between high and low water mark and had cut sedge "thereon; and it was held that this was not such an "occupation of the land as would support a defense "of adverse possession." (McFarlane vs. Kerr, 10 Bosw. 249.)

"In order to make good a claim of title by ad-
"verse holding, the true owner must have actual
"knowledge of the hostile claim, or the possession
"must be so open, visible and notorious as to raise
"the presumption of notice to the world that the
"right of the true owner is invaded intentionally and
"with a purpose to assert a claim of title adversely
"to his, so patent that the owner could not be de-
"ceived and such that if he remains in ignorance it is
"his own fault. A clandestine entry or possession
"will not set the Statute in motion. The owner will
"not be condemned to lose his land because he has
"failed to sue for its recovery, when he had no no-
"tice that it was held or claimed adversely." (Cyl.
Vol. I, 997.)

"There must therefore be a continuous *oc-*
"*cupation* and possession of the premises in-
"cluded in the instrument or some part thereof
"for twenty years.

"There must, however, be an *occupant,* not
"necessarily of the entire tract, but of some part
"of the land claimed to be held adversely."

"The *possession* and *occupation* referred to
"in the section of the Code is *actual occupation*
"of the premises or of some part of them and
"*not* the *occasional* going upon the premises for
"the purpose of cutting wood, and drawing it off.
"These acts do not constitute occupation and
"possession of any part of the premises. *They*
"*partake rather of the nature of trespass on real*
"*property.*"

"To constitute adverse possession the Legis-

"lature contemplates an *actual* and *continued* oc-
"cupation of at least *some part* of the premises
"*under a claim of title to it all* and where there
"has been no actual *occupation* of any part and
"*no inclosing,* there can be *no constructive ad-*
"*verse possession.*" (Wiechers vs. McCormick,
122 N. Y. Ap. 860.)

"Whatever was done upon it was to take value
"from it, not to put value into it. . . . Payment of
"taxes, surveying and assertion of right do not con-
"stitute possession. . . . Going upon land from
"time to time and cutting logs thereon, does not give
"possession. Such acts are merely trespasses upon
"the land against the true owner, whoever he may
"be. Any other intruder may commit similar tres-
"passes without liability to any other trespasser.
"Such acts do not constitute a disseizin of the true
"owner." (Thompson vs. Burhans, 79 N. Y. 93.)

"A person cannot acquire title to an uninclosed,
"unoccupied, unimproved parcel of land by taking a
"deed thereof from one not the owner and then
"merely going upon the land and there asserting his
"ownership, nor can he acquire the title by taking
"such a deed and then making an occasional foray
"upon the land for grass or sand and thus com-
"mitting trespass against the real owner." (Miller
vs. L. I. R. R. Co., 71 N. Y. 380.)

He who takes record title in descent from one
whom he believes acquired his title by adverse possession must be able to prove the hostile intent of his
predecessor in possession. It will not be sufficient to

show that such predecessor held possession for the period prescribed in the Statute. He may have held under a lease or other instrument not hostile to the true owner.

It must be shown by actual proof that for each year during the whole term such possession was held in an open, notorious and hostile manner, adverse to the true owner and with all the conditions requisite thereto.

Such proof is extremely difficult and rarely possible to obtain even where the facts are consistent with such a theory.

It is one thing to know a fact and another thing to prove the same without flaw and to the satisfaction of a Court, especially where the theory is repugnant to justice. In consequence thereof, the law is strictly construed.

THE LARGER VISION

CROWN GRANTS

He who takes title to lands, takes it subject to all of the prior conditions and restrictions imposed of record thereon.

"Assuming the King to be the source of "all titles both of dignity and property. Grants "of land from him to his chieftains were made "in consideration of military service to him- "self, i. e., the Crown, whenever required.

"These direct Grantees of the Crown, ten- "ants in chief or *in capite,* as they were styled, "parceled out their Grants among their follow- "ers or vassals, for like considerations of "Knight service to themselves as *mesne* lords "and these again to inferior persons in consid- "eration of various kinds of service.

"Every land tenure of the kingdom was thus "linked with and dependent on its immediate "superior Grant, all culminating in the King "as the Lord paramount and military chief of "the State."

It will therefore be observed that each and every sub-proprietor, through succeeding generations, who took title to and entered upon any portion of the lands covered and conveyed under an original Crown Grant, acquired possession thereof under the restrictions and limitations of the original foudation Grant from the Sovereign.

In the opening chapter of this book we have undertaken to show how modern title searchers in tracing back through the records of the past generations, the descent of titles as they have come down to us from generations now gone, have laboriously found their way to human Sovereigns as the original source of all land titles.

They have halted at the throne of worldly monarchs and have noted as final and conclusive the conditions of title imposed by earthly kings. They have largely if not totally failed to discover and apply the fundamentally controlling conditions clearly and emphatically recorded in the *Great Book of Records* of the original Crown Grant made by the *King of all the Earth,* i. e., the Book of all Books—the Bible—the Word of God.

The basic conditions therein prescribed, if violated, carried their own penalties. The divine right of reentry and confiscation are therein clearly reserved, as against all Grantees who lack fealty and service to the Great King.

The Sub-Grants made thereunder, by human Sovereigns and all of the subsequent deeds and conveyances by individuals to individuals, despite their "warrantys," admit of no possible unrestricted and unconditional titles as vested in any citizen, to any land in any portion of the habitable world.

All lands which are claimed to be privately owned are in fact, consciously or unconsciously, held subject to clearly defined conditions of fealty and service to the World's Great Sovereign, which conditions are fully recorded in the Record of the Original Crown Grant referred to above.

Such obligations "run with the land."

Human kings recognize, (though in practice they may disregard) these original and governing conditions, when they assert the "divine right of Kings." They thereby claim special dignity and rights of property by Divine Charter. They therefore cannot logically deny the force and effect of the conditions imposed thereby.

There are certain implied and expressed rights and privileges which attach to and descend with each and every Grant to land from such a beneficient and truly Royal source, even though such implied rights are not engrossed in the language of each of the conveyances.

These rights are confirmed by the divinely inspired Magna Charta of the Great King's Realm and are enjoyed by the worthy Grantees under the common law of Divine beneficience. Very solemn obligations also attach thereto. Human Judges have recognized such Divinely ordained rights of common humanity, while a Christian civilization has rediscovered the conditions imposed upon rights of ownership. The conditions prescribed are Fealty and Service, under the moral or common law of righteousness.

The right to the air we breathe, the waters we navigate, together with the sunshine we enjoy, are rights common to all humanity and are inalienable.

One Grantee may not deprive another Grantee of either one or more of such rights.

He who is at the source of a stream of water may not divert the same to his neighbor's hurt.

He who chooses to operate a manufacturing plant must so conduct the same as not to pollute his neighbors' air or the water he drinks.

The popular appreciation of certain equitable or moral rights is happily transforming human laws and the spirit of fraternity is coming forth, more and more, to full flower and fruitage.

In the toilsome upward climb of human life, toward higher planes of thinking, so-called "property rights" are becoming more and more subject to the great moral principles or mandatory laws of the Divine Sovereign proclaimed by Him for controlling and governing all human relations.

In distress, one human, though a stranger to the land owner, may trespass without penalty upon his neighbor's land.

A man famishing with hunger, may rightfully demand bread from his next-of-kin and even of the community at large.

The possession of power gives no right to the strong to oppress the weak, but on the contrary *imposes a peculiar moral responsibility* to succor and defend the needy.

This principle, public conscience now admits, holds good whether such power is represented by miiltary weapons, consists of physical strength or is inherent in the ownership of lands on which others depend for life, health and happiness.

Science cannot isolate and exhibit in tangible form that which constitutes the law of gravitation, which law holds its sway in all organic matter. Neither can we disassociate and visualize the moral elements in human relations.

These elements when codified in action represent the great, though erstwhile dormant laws with which human society, from its very concept has been charged.

The human race is forging ahead to the acceptance of the true theory of Divine Sovereignty and is catching anew, with increased light, the vision of original Divine proprietorship. Temporary but conditional human possession of land is to be followed by ultimate possession by the Creator of all things. His statutes are right, His laws are just. Having out of His marvelous beneficence, issued to us His Royal Grant, He doth require that we too shall be likewise benefactors. While powers of administration are possessed, the true Grantee will not forget his final accountability for the use to which he puts that of which he has been made God's trustee for the benefit of his fellow man.

A new conviction of moral right and obligation is being formed. This is especially true of the moral rights and obligations existing between fellow Grantees and also between those who may and those may not be able to trace back their land titles, without a break in the chain of record, to the Great Original Source of all titles, *but whose geneology extends back to the same Father's House.*

This linking of property rights to the true and only Original Source of all titles and the full and complete recognition of the solemn conditions imposed thereon by the Royal Grant, is transforming proprietorship into stewardship and is smoothing life's rough pathways to many weary feet, which in their toilsome wanderings have trespassed upon the rights in lands of others.

The defiant cry of the original terror stricken Cain, "Am I my brother's keeper?" was but the unconscious outcry of a great moral protest within him which he sought to smother, but which burst forth to stir the consciences of men for all time to come.

Wheeled vehicles, according to city ordinances, may not travel on public sidewalks, but the cripple may, with perfect impunity, roll his invalid's chair thereon, under the higher law which makes its appeal to manly strength and moral consciousness.

All traffic, despite statute laws, must cease, while speed limits are disregarded, as the rushing ambulance carries its burden of suffering to the hospital built by strangers from revenues arbitrarily assessed as "quit-rents" or taxes on lands generally claimed by private individuals as owned by them in fee.

He who but admits that original proprietorship and ultimate ownership of all land is vested in the Divine Sovereign, back and above human sovereigns (and who can deny it?) must then accept its corollary that human relations are those of brotherhood, and that stewardship is a true substitute for the false doctrine of personal, unconditional, unrestricted and selfish ownership of land and other property.

He who may have unwittingly trespassed upon another's land finds under this doctrine fraternity and not hostility in his efforts to amend the wrong.

The great corporations, which through error may have extended their tracks and constructed their warehouses, factories and docks on lands not their own, may unhesitatingly make their appeal for rightful consideration, at the bar of equity in the court of inner conscience where moral law reigns supreme.

Where such trespass has resulted in the enhancement of values to remaining lands by virtue of such added improvements having been placed adjacent thereto, then equity should consider the values of such increment, in abatement of damages claimed for lands so taken in error of judgment or in consequence of faulty surveys.

The moral law by divine mandate "runs with the land," and its demand for equity and justice may not be claimed by one and yet denied by him to another.

"He who asks equity must do equity."

It may not permit the ruthless tyrants of eviction to lay their cold and remorseless hands upon the gates of "God's acre" in which sleeps the silent forms of the beloved dead.

Conscience, the arbiter of moral law, may decree that temples for divine worship erected by error upon plots of land erroneously supposed to be owned by the devotees at such sacred shrines, shall be exempt from invasion by land claimants.

Other great eleemosynary institutions, which are but generous impulses of human hearts worked out in wood and mortar, may carry out their plans for humanity, unannoyed by processes of eviction.

Equity is but the expression of Divine ideals applied by men in human relations.

This same moral law imposed by Divine beneficence, at the very cradle of the human race, may even insist that weary womanhood and innocent childhood shall find their way to sanded beaches and ocean waters. The gateways to such shores may be closeable under statute law, but may also be held open by those proprietors who hear, heed and obey the mandate of suffering as it speaks by its need to such owners who recognize the conditions of Fealty and Service upon which they but for a short period of time hold land titles in trust for the true Original Proprietor and Ultimate Owner of all things.

They must thus think, who have discovered the governing and controlling conditions inserted by the Original Proprietor and Ultimate Owner of all lands, the-King-of-all-the-Earth, when He issued His Original Crown Grant to the Children of Men.

"What doth the Lord require of thee,

"but to do justly and to love mercy

"and to walk humbly with thy God."

"The Massachusetts Body of Liberties (Section 1) seems to think that * * * if there be no common law or statute for the case, it may be 'by the Word of God,' so Christianity is part of the Common Law."   (Law of the Federal and State Constitution of the U. S., Chap. 6, page 36.)

"Christian Morality is the foundation of international law."—(Cardinal Gasquet, Rome.)

THE SYMES FOUNDATION

AND

CROWN GRANTS

Consistent with the ethical and legal principles hereinbefore set forth and the larger view of true citizenship, which recognizes human interdependence and mutual obligations, the owners of the Lancaster Symes Estate on Staten Island incorporated The Symes Foundation and have transferred to it the lands on Staten Island included therein.

We give in the following order a transcript of the record covering the dedication to the public weal of the Symes Estate, with its very large and increasing values descending under and from the English Crown Grant to Lancaster Symes.

> Section 1.—Letter from the Title Companies to the citizens and friends of Staten Island.
>
> Section 2.—Certificate of Incorporation of The Symes Foundation.
>
> Section 3.—Contract between the American Title and Trust Company and The Symes Foundation.

These citations reveal the fact that after two centuries the Life and Character of Major Lancaster Symes has found full appreciation and the Estate on Staten Island which he gathered together as a loyal subject and Christian citizen has been set apart in a manner to make it a lasting blessing to Staten Island, of which he was a benefactor and to America, to which he came from England and to which he devoted his life.

Section 1.

AMERICAN TITLE AND SECURITY COMPANY, AMERICAN TITLE AND TRUST COMPANY

And

THE SYMES FOUNDATION, INCORPORATED.
"STATEN ISLAND FOR STATEN ISLANDERS."
Richmond, Staten Island, N. Y.
July 2nd, 1917.

TO THE CITIZENS AND FRIENDS OF STATEN ISLAND:
After years of costly and laborious research conducted by specialists in England and America, the undersigned title companies under the direction of their President, Mr. S. L. Mershon, have clearly defined and definitely located, from official maps and records, all of the lands on Staten Island originally granted to Major Lancaster Symes under the English Crown Grant made to him in 1708 and duly recorded at Albany, New York.

The regularity and binding force and effect of the said grant has never been called in question in any legal proceedings, but on the contrary it has been admitted, ratified and confirmed by the Province of New York, the State of New York, eminent railway and other corporate and private counsel. Upon it rests and from it descends the title to various lands of great value on Staten Island upon which costly ecclesiastical, residential and commercial improvements have been erected and for which many warranty deeds have been issued and approved for generations and which have never been challenged by any title companies, mortgage companies or private counsel. The titles so referred to are acceptable to savings banks, building loan associations and other organizations for loans thereon.

St. Andrews Protestant Episcopal Church at Richmond, Staten Island, received its endowment deed direct from Major Lancaster Symes, who received his title from Queen Anne, "The good Queen" of England.

For generations, however, a cloud has rested upon large areas of land on Staten Island because of the uncertainty in the popular mind as well as in the legal mind as to what lands, other than those known to be, were covered by and included in the Symes title.

To this problem the undersigned two title companies have successfully devoted their untiring efforts and financial resources with the result that such clouds of uncertainty and doubt have been completely dispelled.

From the commencement of this investigation by these two title companies they have at all times kept clearly in view the eventual free release of the homesteads of Staten Island from the shadow whether justly or unjustly cast upon such homes by the Symes Grant. They have at all times intended to free the religious and charitable institutions on Staten Island from the lien of this Grant and to open up under proper moral control, certain beaches on Staten Island for free use and enjoyment by Staten Islanders and their friends. These and other benefits should make the Symes Grant a blessing to Staten Island for all time to come.

In fulfilment of this ambitious program the two title companies now voluntarily and with great pleasure pass over to The Symes Foundation, which they have established and endowed, a good, complete and perfect title to the lands now remaining of record in Richmond County in the name of the American Title and Trust Company.

Such title cannot be successfully challenged or assailed and is good and sufficient in The Symes Foundation and to the defense of which the two undersigned title companies pledge their unqualified support at any time upon demand.

The control of this entire estate now passes into the hands of the representatives of Staten Island through The Symes Foundation but charged with one supreme and sacred trust, that it will be used at all times for the highest and best good of Staten Island and its people as set forth in a contract, governing such use and executed between the undersigned and The Symes Foundation.

In addition thereto provision has been made by the two title companies for a large and increasing financial endowment for the Symes Foundation, which should result in unmeasurable benefits to the public.

Respectfully,
S. L. MERSHON, President,
AMERICAN TITLE & SECURITY CO.
Richmond, Staten Island.

AMERICAN TITLE & TRUST CO.
Wilmington, Delaware.

Section 2.

CERTIFICATE OF INCORPORATION.

THE SYMES FOUNDATION, INC.

We, the undersigned, all being persons of full age and all or more than two-thirds of us being citizens of the United States and all or more than one, being residents of the State of New York, desiring to form a corporation for benevolent and charitable work, do hereby and pursuant to sections 40 and 41 of the Membership Corporations Law of the State of New York make, sign and acknowledge this certificate as follows :—

First, the name of the proposed corporation is The Symes Foundation, Inc.

Second, the purposes of the Corporation are (1) to take title to and ownership of certain lands, premises, rights and privileges represented by and existent under the "Lancaster Symes Grant," which rights and interests are now vested in and exercised by the American Title and Trust Company, a Delaware Corporation with its principal office in the

Dupont Building, Wilmington, Delaware; (2) to hold the same in fee, to sell and convey any part or parts, to devote to public use any part or parts; (3) to use such proceeds as may be available from said sale or otherwise together with any portion of said properties reserved and held to promote and develop the physical, mental, moral and spiritual welfare of the people of Staten Island and elsewhere, (a) by furnishing to the people of Staten Island certain bathing beaches, (b) by erecting thereon, equipping and sustaining fresh-air camps and lodges, hospitals, rest cures, and hotels for the benefit and recuperation of those needing such, (c) by conducting what is commonly known as Chautauqua courses; by operating moving pictures and other proper and lawful pleasure-giving and instructive amusements; by conducting and maintaining musical, literary, gospel, and evangelistic services, which shall in every case be without admission fee and free to the people (d) providing free pavilions and making all such other improvements as may be deemed necessary, desirable or convenient for carrying out the purposes and objects of this corporation, (e) to lay out, beautify and improve parks, drives, roadways, board-walks on the seashores and to do each and everything proper both expressed and implied in the foregoing which may be deemed desirable to aid this corporation in promoting and developing the benevolent work for which it is organized.

Third, the County within which its operations are to be conducted is Richmond County, New York State.

Fourth, the principal office is to be located in the

Borough of Manhattan, in the County of New York and State of New York.

Fifth, the number of its directors is five.

Sixth, the names and places of residence of the persons to be its directors until its first annual meeting are as follows:

Charles D. Durkee..Rosebank, N. Y.
John E. Fisher.....Rosebank, N. Y.
S. L. Mershon......Montclair, N. J.
Frank Hamilton....Richmond, N. Y.
Robert G. Davey..203 Broadway, N. Y.

Seventh, the time for holding the annual meeting is on the first Monday of October in each year.

IN WITNESS WHEREOF, we have made, signed and acknowledged this certificate, dated this 12th day of June, 1917.

Charles D. Durkee...819 Fingerboard Road, S. I.
John E. Fisher......71 Central Ave.
S. L. Mershon.......28 Forrest St.
Frank Hamilton...Andrews Ave., Richmond, S. I.
Robert G. Davey....404 E. 141st St., N. Y. C.

STATE OF NEW YORK,
County of New York, ss.

On this 12th day of June, 1917, before me personally came

CHARLES D. DURKEE
JOHN E. FISHER
S. L. MERSHON
FRANK HAMILTON
ROBERT G. DAVEY

To me known and known to me to be the persons described in and who executed the foregoing certificate and severally and duly acknowledged to me that they executed the same.

(Signed) PETER F. WIESE
Notary Public
Kings County
Kings County Clerks No. 121
N. Y. Co. Clerks No. 382
N. Y. Register's No. 8247
Commission expires Mar. 30, 1918.

I, the undersigned, Justice of the Supreme Court of the State of New York, do hereby approve of the within certificate. Dated at the city of New York, County of Kings, this 22nd day of June, 1917.

CHARLES H. KELBY
Justice of the Supreme Court
of the State of New York.

STATE OF NEW YORK,
County of New York, ss.

On this 12th day of June, 1917, before me came John E. Fisher of New York, Charles D. Durkee of New York and Robert G. Davey of New York, personally known to me and known to be the parties whose names appear as directors of the foregoingCertificate of Incorporation, and being duly

sworn they severally declared that they were citizens
of the United States of America.

(Signed) PETER F. WIESE
Notary Public
Kings County
Kings County Clerk's No. 121
N. Y. Co. Clerk s No. 382
N. Y. Registers No. 8247
Commission expires Mar. 30, 1918.

Section 3.

CONTRACT.

AMERICAN TITLE AND TRUST CO.

WITH

THE SYMES FOUNDATION.

This contract made and entered into this 30th day
of June, 1917, in the City of Wilmington, State of
Delaware, by and between the American Title and
Trust Company, a Delaware Corporation with its
principal office in the Dupont Building in the aforesaid city and state, its successors and assigns party
of the First Part and The Symes Foundation, Inc.,
a New York Corporation with its principal office in
the Borough of Manhattan in the City and State
of New York, its successors and assigns, party of
the Second Part.

WITNESSETH THAT,

WHEREAS the party of the first part is the record owner of certain of the rights, title and interests now remaining unconveyed by it, in and to certain lands and premises commonly known as the English Crown Grant to Lancaster Symes; said lands and premises being situated in and extending to the bounds and limits of the County of Richmond in the State of New York and which said English Crown Grant appears of record in the office of the Secretary of State at Albany, New York, in the Book of Records of Patents, Volume 7, pages 411, 412, and 413, and also appears of record in the office of the County Clerk of the said County of Richmond and to which records reference is hereby made for a more accurate description thereof and also as shown on a certain map of said English Crown Grants on Staten Island in said Richmond County and which map is to be recorded in the said County Clerk's office at Richmond, Staten Island, and is entitled "Symes Foundation map of English Crown Grants No. 1."

Whereas the State of New York did commute the quit rents payable under the aforesaid Lancaster Symes Grant, as does appear of record in the Record Book of Quit Rents, Docket 48, page 106 in the Comptroller's Office at Albany, in the State of New York, thereby ratifying, confirming and establishing forever and in effect issuing a new Grant and title in fee thereunder in the successors of Record Title to the said Lancaster Symes, and

Whereas the State of New York did, on the

twelfth day of September, 1877, disavow any title in and to the said Lancaster Symes Grant and Lands as appears of record in the correspondence book or letter file in the office of the Secretary of State at Albany, New York, and in the following language, to wit:—

> "We have no knowledge of any lands be-
> "longing to the State on Staten Island. In 1708
> "a Grant was made to Lancaster Symes, of all
> "and every piece and parcel of vacant and un-
> "appropriated land and meadow on Staten
> "Island. Many letters are received at this office
> 'relative to the title of occupants on the Island
> 'and lands supposed to be owned by the State,
> "but we can furnish no information except the
> "Grants which appear upon our records," and

Whereas the map hereinbefore referred to is a correct tracing from a map made and prepared by direction of the Hon. Secretary of State at Albany, and which said map was ordered so made by, was drawn for, was submitted to and was filed with the said Hon. Secretary of State by the then State Engineer and the then State Surveyor under the official direction and command of the said Secretary of State. And a blueprint of the said map printed from the original of the said map so prepared by the said State Officers and employees was delivered at the office of the Secretary of State at Albany to the first party hereto, the said blueprint having been made in the State Engineer's office in Albany for First Party by direct order from the Secretary of State's office and delivered at the office of the Secretary of State to First Party and said blueprint shows the location of each and every portion of said English Crown Grant made to lands on Staten Island as aforesaid to Lancaster Symes, excepting only, however that the said map and blueprint thereof do not show the bounds and limits of Richmond County set forth in the said Grant as the bounds and limits thereof, and the said map furthermore shows and was expressly made intending to show the vacant and unappropriated lands granted as aforesaid to Lancaster Symes, the said Grant covering and including among other things "meadows, marshes, swamps, pools, ponds, waters, water-courses, rivers, rivoletts, runs and streams of water" . . . within "the bounds and limits of Richmond County" as set forth in the aforesaid English Crown Grant to Lancaster Symes, and

Whereas the First Party recognizes the fact that there are many rights belonging to the public which are not specifically comprehended in the statutes of the State of New York, and that such truly equitable rights frequently are not obtainable by the public through an action either at law or in equity but are only to be possessed and enjoyed by the people when the same are voluntarily accorded or surrendered by those from whom the same are morally due to the community under the higher law of righteousness, under which law of righteousness human needs both individual and communal dictate to the awakened conscience, the true rule of action, and

WHEREAS the possessory rights of large areas of the landed estate included under the aforesaid Lancaster Symes Grant, may have in fact passed from first party, by the possession of parties now holding adversely to the original and record owners thereof, to the impairment of said estate, but the proofs of which adverse possession are difficult to establish and largely non-procurable by such parties in adverse possession and whereas a large number of good and law-abiding citizens residing with their families on Staten Island, relying and depending upon such adverse possession and lacking sufficient proofs thereof as required by law to sustain what has become and is now their lawful possession thereof, would be dprieved of their present actual legal rights thereto to their great loss and hurt by and in the event of first party's successfully invoking the law for their eviction, and

WHEREAS many law-abiding and industrious citizens of Staten Island have innocently taken possession of lands included in, and which are now actually covered by, the Lancaster Symes title, have paid to supposedly the actual owners thereof, substantially full value therefor and have thereby fully believed themselves to have become the actual owners thereof, and to whom a process of eviction would mean financial ruin and irreparable disaster, and

WHEREAS the First Party believes that any such wholesale evictions though legal in character would be and constitute a public calamity, would entail great individual suffering and loss, and would adversely affect the entire community, and whereas First Party further believes that a happy, contented homelife is a community's largest asset and should be protected and safe-guarded at almost any cost of private interests and especially by corporations created by public permission, favor, and consent, and which are intended to operate for private gain consistent only with the public welfare, and

WHEREAS the First Party believes that Philanthropic Eleemosenary and Religious Institutions are the highest expressions of human activity in a Christian Civilization and should be immune as far as possible from all controversy and claims which would impair their potency for the public weal especially where such claims are possessed by parties who recognize the welfare of the public as paramount to extraordinary gain to those who "have enough and to spare" and especially where possessed by corporations whose property values and commercial prosperity are measurably dependent upon the existence and maintenance of such institutions, and

WHEREAS the First Party, moved by the considerations hereinbefore expressed, has inspired by its suggestion and has directed the organization and incorporation of Second Party hereto and Second Party hereto has become a corporate body under the laws of the State of New York with full powers for its complete performance hereunder and as provided herein, and

WHEREAS the parties hereto mutually and severally desire that the property rights and privileges aforesaid which are situated within the bounds and limits of said Richmond County and which are owned and possessed by the first party hereto, shall be and become controlled, managed, leased or sold as herein provided and the proceeds thereof largely devoted and applied for the physical, mental, moral

and spiritual betterment of Staten Island for all
time to come

Now THEREFORE, the parties hereto moved by
such unity of purpose and harmony in conclusions
hereinbefore expressed and further, in consideration of the circumspect and unselfish attitude of
the people of Staten Island toward the First Party
hereto pending First Party's assertion and development of proof of its right and title to the properties covered by and included in the Lancaster
Symes English Crown Grant and further in consideration of those higher and holier claims that
rest upon each member of the social order in our
Christian civilization to seek the highest happiness
and greatest good of the individual and of the community at large and for other valuable considerations, the adequacy and receipt of which the parties
hereto, herein admit and declare, the First and Second parties hereto mutually and severally agree as
follows, to wit:—

I.

The First Party hereto does hereby grant, assign,
transfer, release and convey to the party of the
Second Part all of first party's rights, title claims
and interest now remaining in, to and under the
aforementioned English Crown Grant to Lancaster
Symes to lands and other values not heretofore conveyed by First Party within the bounds and limits
of Richmond County in the State of New York as
said Grant is shown in the Records in the office
of the Secretary of State at Albany and in the

office of the County Clerk of Richmond County, New York, and as shown on the aforementioned and described map and as contained within the said bounds and limits of Richmond County as such bounds and limits are now constituted and defined and as they were constituted and defined at the time of the issue by the English Crown of the aforementioned English Crown Grant to Lancaster Symes. This transfer and conveyance is absolute and without reservation. The proceeds from the sale, leasing or operation of the properties herein referred to are subject only to the terms and conditions herein provided; the lands conveyed to Second Party as aforesaid are absolutely free of any lien upon or ownership therein reserved to first party.

II.

The Second Party hereto shall forthwith, or as soon hereafter as it may find the same to be reasonably practicable, release by quit claim under the said Symes Grant upon satisfactory application being made to it therefor, the following classes of lands or properties on Staten Island and within said Richmond County, to wit:—

(*a*) Each and every Church property or place of worship that is devoted to the worship of Almighty God and the Record title to which is held by a duly accredited reliigous organization legally incorporated and conducting or sanctioning such worship with proper authority and right so to do.

(*b*) Every piece of land on which is erected an

institution devoted to human uplift, supported entirely or substantially so by philanthropy or charity.
In this class shall be included:—

(1) Schools.
(2) Children's homes, orphan asylums and homes for the aged and infirm.
(3) Hospitals.
(4) Asylums.

excepting only however, that Second Party may at its discretion decline to consider as included herein or may from time to time elect to include herein institutions supported by public taxation.

(c) Burial grounds or cemeteries which are under religious auspices and ownership and which are operated, controlled and possessed by corporations organized to be conducted without profit.

All family burial places are to be included hereunder unless in the judgment of Second Party, certain burial places should be omitted because of indefinite or uncertain locations or for other reasons approved by the judgment and conscience of Second Party.

(d) The homes and homesteads of Staten Island shall be released by Second Party from the lien or claim of the Lancaster Symes Grant, to such an extent and in such instances as the judgment of the Second Party may dictate. It is the desire of First Party hereto that the homelife of Staten Island as now existing in its present homesteads shall be forever free of any and all claims or shadow of claims under the said Symes Grant. Which homesteads are and which are not entitled to such release shall be determined, however, by Second Party. While Second Party is hereby clothed with discretionary power to decide and determine in each case the merits of each claim for releasement hereunder, the first party hereto, hereby solemnly charges the second party at all times to consider well the First Party's wishes in this matter and to discriminate adversely only where such adverse discrimination, in Second Party's judgment is truly equitable and will not prove to be financially burdensome or which discrimination is otherwise fully justified under the spirit of this instrument.

III.

Certain beaches or shore fronts adapted for public bathing places shall be set apart at the judgment and discretion of Second Party for the benefits of the public at large. Such beaches shall be selected designated and so appropriated at times and locations approved by the judgment of Second Party. Such beaches shall be under the management of Second Party or parties designated and appointed by Second Party and shall be free to the public subject only to such limitations and restrictions as may be from time to time considered desirable and best and which shall be prescribed by Second Party for the proper maintenance, improvement and development of the same. Second Party may keep and maintain such beaches in perpetuity for the welfare of the public or may change and remove such public privileges and facilities from one location to another location as in the judgment of the Second Party shall best serve the public, or it may from time to time regulate and restrict the same as in its judgment may best serve the highest good of the public.

This provision is intended to restore to the citizens of Staten Island and to those who seek its shores adequate bathing beaches and beneficial pleasure resorts well regulated under strict moral control and management and where health and happiness shall be promoted by equipment and appliancees calculated for physical development, mental entertainment and spiritual instruction.

It is intended hereby that God's free air and His ocean tides on Staten Island shores shall be the portion of the citizens as freely as the judgment and discretion of Second Party hereto may so supply the same under proper regulations substantially if not absolutely without money and without price and under pleasure producing and character building influences consistent with the teachings of Jesus Christ.

IV.

First Party having been advised by counsel and citizens of Staten Island that certain parties have trespassed upon certain of the aforesaid lands situated on what is commonly known as Lake Island (which Lake Island is a portion of Staten Island), have established a garbage plant thereon and are treating or manipulating thereon garbage from other boroughs against the protests of an overwhelming majority of the people of Staten Island and also that certain prominent citizens of Staten Island have been sued at law by certain parties for damages which such parties claim to have suffered from and because of such citizens alleged attempts to restrain the manipulation of said garbage on Staten Island in defiance of the aforementioned public sentiment.

NOW THEREFORE, Second Party shall at its discretion, convey to some representative citizen of Staten Island as trustee to be selected by Second Party, preferably to the President of one of the Staten Island Savings Banks or to a President of a Staten Island Building & Loan Association, all of Second Party's right, title and interest in and to the said Lake Island and its waterfront including the land under water connected therewith extending to the center or thread of Fresh Kill. The said land and water front on Lake Island if and when so conveyed may be sold by said trustee if deemed by him necessary to compensate or financially protect said citizens, so sued as aforesaid, in the event of a decree against said citizens in the above mentioned suit or to defray the expenses of the Second Party or of Second Party and said citizens in contesting the right of said parties so to occupy and possess Lake Island or any part thereof as aforesaid or to manufacture or treat garbage at any place on Staten Island, all however subject to such terms, conditions and restrictions as Second Party may deem proper to stipulate in the premises. Full discretion is hereby expressly given to Second Party under this Section.

V.

As the lands or properties hereinbefore referred

to are of a varied nature or are of a diversified character and as it may prove difficult at all times to determine who may or who may not, be entitled to the benefits intended to be granted as aforesaid under Section II hereof or what property or properties may or may not be included or intended to be included in any one or more of the foregoing classifications and as the right and power to make such determination should and must rest and abide somewhere; the Party of the Second Part is to have the final and exclusive right hereunder to settle and determine the same according to its best judgment if and as any uncertainty may, from time to time arise, or when and as any uncertainty or controversy relating thereto arises, anything contained herein to the contrary notwithstanding. Such decision or decisions made by Second Party from time to time shall be final, conclusive and binding upon all parties hereto or claiming hereunder. Such decisions may be reversed, rescinded, or modified at any time thereafter by Second Party if it deems such reversal, decision or modification to be equitable and proper, but not where the titles subject to such decision have passed from Second Party to other parties in the meantime.

VI.

Second Party may make such nominal charges as it may from time to time deem to be proper, proportionate, appropriate and sufficient, to cover Second Party's actual cost in releasing the properties or lands referred to herein and may make such charges in each case or in any case, a condition precedent to the making of such release or releases or Second Party may at its discretion waive any and all such charges and costs or may make any charges therefor as it may consider equitable or suited to the conditions of the applicant. It is not intended that any profits shall be made by Second Party from such charges but it is intended that Second Party may charge what it believes to be its fair average cost or its cost in the particular cases. The Second Party is to have absolute authority to fix such rates from time to time and such rates or schedule of rates shall be final until altered or changed by Second Party.

VII.

No action shall be taken by Second Party in any matter relating to any release of property hereunder in which property any director or officer of Second Party is personally interested as claimant unless such director or officer is absent or withdraws from the meeting at which such proposed action is taken and during the final discussion thereof at such meeting and at which meeting the question is fully discussed and is so reported on the minutes of such meeting as to have been finally discussed and voted on in the absence of such claimant. No director shall vote on any matter particularly relating to property in which he or his immediate family is known by him to be financially interested as an owner or claimant thereto.

VIII.

The First Party waives any and all right to receive any further payment from Second Party from any properties or land granted or leased by Second Party for a nominal consideration only, under Section II hereof as specified in subdivisions *a, b, c, d, e, f,* of said Section II.   All deeds granted by The Symes Foundation shall be Quit Claim, and shall be conditioned to prohibit forever the use of lands affected for the manufacture or sale of alcoholic beverages or liquors.

IX.

Second Party is to account in detail and pay to First Party one-half of all money received by Second Party from the sale, leasing or other business done by Second Party with any of the lands, etc. herein mentioned which may be sold, leased, or operated by Second Party excepting as otherwise herein provided.   Such accountings and payments are to be made by Second Party to First Party on the first day of each and every January, April, July and October of each and every year.   Such payments shall be accompanied by proper credit vouchers duly audited, but Second Party shall not be required hereunder to pay to First Party any of the nominal fees charged for properties released under Section II hereof.

Any and all funds collected by Second Party hereto on or between the dates designated herein and which funds under the terms hereof are to be and become payable to First Party hereto are to be de-

posited in Banks or Trust Companies designated
from time to time by the party of the First Part
and which Banks or Trust Companies shall be approved by and be in good standing with the bank-
ing department of the state in which the same is
located. When such funds are so deposited in said
banks or trust companies they shall be there so
held until the proper date of payment thereof to
First Party at the risk of First Party or all or a
part thereof may be paid to First Party by Second
Party prior to such date.

The remaining one-half of such moneys so received by Second Party from the sale, leasing or
operation of the aforesaid properties is to be used
by Second Party on Staten Island for Second Party's
operating expenses and for the establishment of institutions and equipment intended by Second Party
to secure the physical, mental, moral and spiritual
betterment of the public. The form and manner
of such expenditure and use shall be such as in the
judgment of the Second Party will be consistent
with the principles and teachings of Jesus Christ.
Such expenditures may take the form of beach improvements; educational and religious instruction,
the erection and maintenance of a tabernacle for
interdenominational religious services, conventions
and other assemblies; the construction and maintenance of hotels for self-supporting young women
and others, the same to be operated at cost; the
building of bungalows for rentals at so near cost
as Second Party can determine; the equipment of
tennis courts; the supplying of bathing facilities and
other proper comforts and conveniences for the happiness of and benefits to the public; the maintenance

of what is known as fresh air work for women and children and said expenditures may take such other forms as Second Party may deem to be in accordance with, the true intent of this instrument.

First Party shall have the right at any and all reasonable times to inspect the books of Second Party and to have the same at any time audited by auditors employed by First Party at its own expense in order that First Party may be at all times satisfied with the system and methods employed by Second Party in keeping such accounts. Such accounts shall be at all times well and properly kept by Second Party.

X.

Nothing contained herein shall be construed as even implying that Second Party shall not use a proportion of its segregated income from the aforesaid proceeds, for the payment of its general expenses incurred by it in the operation of its affairs other than those actually incurred on Staten Island. It is itnended, however, that all incomes accruing hereunder to Second Party as afore provided are to be used in the payment of Second Party's expenses of administration and are to be preferably invested and expended on tSaten Island as aforesaid, according to the judgment and discretion of Second Party. In no event shall any such incomes to Second Party be construed to be or constitute a commercial profit or dividend payable to or to be distributed among any members or shareholders in Second Party or for any distribution other than herein provided. The amount to be paid to the

officers, employees, and directors of Second Party
as aforesaid is to be determined from time to time
by the best judgment of the said directors as proper
and fair compensation for actual personal services
rendered therefor, entirely apart from and independent of any vested interest which any such party
or parties may have in Second Party.

XI.

Second Party shall only be liable hereunder for
any expenditures and investments made according
to the exercise from time to time by Second Party's
officers and directors of their best judgment in the
premises. The First Party hereto declines to hold
Second Party's officers and trustees to personal liability hereunder for any errors or mistakes of judgment made by them while in the performance of
services rendered under this sacred trust.

XII.

Second Party may invest, preferably on Staten
Island, any funds which it may be entitled to and
does receive under its allotment of one-half of the
incomes hereunder if it desires so to do and by
such investment undertakes to create a reserve or
interest bearing fund for the carrying out of the
purposes hereof. In such events such investments
so made shall be made in accordance with the best
judgment of the directors and when so made, no
further obligation or liability shall rest upon the
directors for the safety of such investment.

It is the desire of the first party, though not

required hereby, that Second Party shall seek to so invest or loan from time to time portions of suc' funds at low rates of interest as will enable the worthy laboring classes to erect their own homes on Staten Island according to plans approved by the Second Party.

XIII.

In order that the true intent of this instrument may be carried out in perpetuity, it is stipulated by the First Party, and accepted by Second Party;

First, that the incorporating members of The Symes Foundation and the first or original Board of Directors thereof shall be five.

Second, that the first or original Board of Directors shall continue in office and shall have power to choose and elect a director to fill any vacancy or vacanies therein from whatever cause, for and during the period of two years from the date of the execution of this instrument and until their successors are duly elected and qualified.

Third, that on or before the expiration of the said period of two years, according to the judgment so expressed by either party hereto the Board of Directors of Second Party shall be increased to seventeen members to be selected in the following manner, to wit:—

The then existing Board of Directors shall choose and elect two laymen who shall be officials in the Reformed (Dutch) Church of Staten Island or members thereof approved by two of its pastors; two who shall be officials in the Methodist Episcopal Church of Staten Island or members thereof approved by two of its pastors; one who shall be an official in the Protestant Episcopal Church of Staten Island or a member thereof approved by one of its Rectors; one who shall be an official in the Baptist Church of Staten Island or a member thereof approved by one of its pastors; and one who shall be an official in the Moravian Church of Staten Island or a member thereof approved by one of its pastors; and one who shall be a member of the Roman Catholic Church. And said existing Board of Directors shall also select nine others who shall be active members or ministers of the Presbyterian Church at least two-thirds of whom shall be laymen, preferably though not of necessity, active elders of the Presbytery of New York; and the Presbytery of New York shall have the right at its discretion to elect or substitute others in the place of all or some of the laymen so selected or to be selected. When the same have been elected and have signified their acceptance in proper form and manner, then these nine persons together with the eight elected as heretofore described, shall constitute the Board of Directors of The Symes Foundation for the ensuing year or until their successors are elected and qualified. This method shall be adopted annually thereafter for the election of Directors. In case of failure on the part of the Presbytery of New York to elect or substitute as aforesaid other directors for the position of Directors of The Symes Foundation, the nine directors named by the then existing Board of Directors shall act as directors for such vacancies for the year in which such failure occurs and for such service until their successors are elected and qualified. The designation of the Presbytery of New York as the organization having power hereunder at any and all elections to cause the election of the majority of the Board of Directors is in no wise intended to make The Symes Foundation a Presbyterian or Sectarian undertaking. The power to control the Foundation in the interest and for the furtherance of the highest ideals in social and economic life must abide and rest under safe control and the Presbytery of New York is designated without prejudice to, but in the interest of and to conserve Christian Catholicity in an Evangelical undertaking operating without personal or private profit in behalf of the public weal.

Should the General Assembly of the Presbyterian Church in the United States of America by proper action and the appointment of a proper committee therefor decide to and does undertake to assume the duties and responsibilities herein set forth and provided to be done and performed by the Presbytery of New York and so notifies second party hereto then the said General Assembly of the Presbyterian Church in the United States of America shall be from that date substituted for the said Presbytery of New York as fully and completely as if it had been so designated and provided in this instrument at its inception and at the time of the execution thereof.

XIV.

The First Party hereto disavows any and every desire on its part to impose any restrictions or binding pledges upon the Directors of The Symes Foundation that would in any wise interfere with the exercise by the said Directors of their unhampered and best judgment as Trustees in the election of its Executive officers. First Party would, however, herein express its opinion that because of special legal training, Christian education and experience together with a keen, close and sympathetic acquaintance on his part with the needs and future possibilities of Staten Island, Robert G. Davey, is specially qualified to act as the President and managing Director of The Symes Foundation. First Party further expresses its opinion that qualification for duty, efficient service, together with health and strength make their own appeal for continuing re-election of a faithful officer.

XV.

It is especially and particularly stipulated and agreed between the Parties hereto anything contained herein to the contrary notwithstanding that if in the course or progress of time any of the restrictions or limitations hereinbefore imposed by First Party are deemed by Second Party to be impractical or in effect hamper and impair the carrying out of the true intent of this instrument then and in that event or at such time or times as such occasion may arise Second Party may make overture to the aforesaid General Assembly of the Presbyterian Church in the United States of America for a modification or cancellation of such restrictions or a temporary suspension thereof and such action which may at such times or times be taken by the said General Assembly, shall be binding and conclusive in the premises and such action or actions is hereby ratified and confirmed in advance and shall have the same force and effect as if the same had been stipulated and included herein at the time of the executiion hereof, but in no such event shall the Evangelical and interdenominational character or spirit of this instrument be impaired.

XVI.

The First Party hereto reiterates its solemn desire and intent that the Second Party shall have and Second Party does hereby receive the lands, claims, rights and properties herein specified, charged with a greaet moral responsibility to use its highest and best judgment in behalf of the health, happiness and welfare of the citizens of Staten Island and the proper and conscientious conservation of all the interests committed to it hereunder by the First Party.

IN WITNESS WHEREOF the parties hereto have caused this instrument to be duly executed by their respective Presidents, duly attested under their corporate seals on the day and year first above written.

AMERICAN TITLE & TRUST COMPANY.

By S. L. MERSHON,

President.

[SEAL]

Attest

WALTER MERRITT BROKAW,

Secretary.

THE SYMES FOUNDATION,

By ROBERT G. DAVEY,

President.

[SEAL]

Attest

J. C. FISHER, Secretary.

INDEX